FIREHEAD

Other books by Lola Ridge

THE GHETTO (1918)

SUN-UP (1920)

RED FLAG (1927)

FIREHEAD

*LOLA
RIDGE*

PAYSON & CLARKE LTD
NEW YORK MCMXXIX

TO YADDO

I wish to thank my many friends whose great kindness during the last two difficult years has made this book possible.

LOLA RIDGE

CONTENTS

FIREHEAD

Marvel that a day, serene as most,
      Should be singled from the anonymous host
      Of days that seem begotten but to weave
Sunlight in old devices on the sand
And pass upon the waters glamorously,
Leaving no trace — save on the youngling rye
And corn and the sweet secret grapes that lean
Big with the juice of festivals, and all
The brave assorted fruitage of the sun
That pay bright homage to oblivion.
Ponder a day as fair as this —
Transfigured now and changed beyond redress —
Smelling of loam and horses and soft airs
Atingle with an April eagerness —
How it was called to stand there in God's way
In stubborn glory, like a golden ass
Forefeet, planted against time, that shall not pass
With light-shod hoofs in darkness. Let there rise
Sands upon its columns infinitely,
Obliterating sands upon its bones,
And on the pillared temples it shall blaze,
Caparisoned, apart from other days.

I
HE

The day was arteried with fire. Beyond
The golden body of the sand
That stretched out torpidly, the sun
Came raging on Jerusalem.
A yelping wind ran with the sand
It lifted like a yellow mane
And cast into his face.

Above him, in the plumbless space
Wherein it seemed no thing could fly,
Against the azure mist there burned
A mote in the sun's eye.
He watched it slowly circling,
No bigger than his hand,
As gracefully it wheeled — a thing
Not swerving claw-breadth as it turned
In gliding circuit from the rim
Indurable, it traced on air,
A lustrous circle, vanishing,
That found its central point in him.

He may have heard a woman wail
Who kneeled far off — upon a mound
In the bright sunshine — like a bird

With white wings folded. If He heard
Or longed to wrap his wounds around
In her blue cooling shadow, she
Had never known by any sign —
Not though his draining heart delayed
One beat . . . to close upon the sound
As a wound closes on a blade.

And when day sank, at menopause,
In blue obesity, to lean
Low upon the curving spine
Of the horizon — at that hour
Stagnate like a knot in time
When no bright gesturings obscure
The changeless core of being — coiled
As in the primal chrysalis —
When light palls and the heart loses
Pride of propelling to such things
As gnaw, unheard, save in imaginings
On under sides of leaves
Or propagate beneath the stones
Or crawl out, wingless, from the slime
Of water holes . . . and nature oozes
At all her pores as with a pus
And torpid flies are venomous —

His spindling body, like a vine
Was stretched as still twixt earth and sky
As anything alive might lie
Between two lions' paws.

He felt the Roman soldiers' reek —
Who spat the highest hit his feet —
He smelled the resin in the cross
As it worked amid the heat.
He smelled the thieves at either hand.
One was old; his sweat was rank;
His ordure dropped upon the sand;
But one smelled of the sea.
The first one cursed him where He lay —
That He could not stay the breeding flies
Nor wipe the sand from out their eyes
Nor take them down from off the Cross —
And cursed the honey-bearing day
With all the host of flying things
That bore its pollen on their wings.
But one cried like an albatross
And he smelled of the sea . . .
Each man suffered his own cross,
Each knew his own agony;

19

But one man wore the rose of pain,
That flowered in each red place, as though
It were some precious thing . . and He
Endured three crosses silently.
Until the sixth hour came He heard
The shriven thieves complain.

The yellow growth of day — yet whole,
Though tremulous, about to fall —
Endured above the ocean . . . wind
Touched him in the old way . . . he saw
Light foam upon Jerusalem,
The golden many braceleted
Jerusalem — to pleasure her,
Before the purple-togaed night
Should lean tiaraed; pridefully
Shroud and bear him from all sight —
Came out from her portals, wearing
Peace, the white lie of the soul,
About her like an aureole . . .
When, curious, she looked on him
Who spun, the pivot of the world,
Erect upon her wheeling skies
The amber light upon her rim
Shone like a lion's eyes.

. . .

Those scribes, who feared the shadow flung
Of that great flame upon the scrolls
On which for daylight they had wrought
To trick the word out, aping thought,
And furbish it, that they likewise
Might glister and their meager souls
Attain more stature in men's eyes,
Picked, of sly habit, warily
From off the oiled quiver of the tongue,
Some sentient dart to cast at him,
There nailed on the horizon's rim,
And climbed to mark him as He hung.

But He
Looked from the crosshead broodingly
Into the fulgent eye of the sun —
They two now level as men of one height,
Bloodshot eye to eye, and met unflinchingly
That inhuman stare, till the horizon rose
And He, its crest, hung gazing on alone.

Gnats stung him and a yellow butterfly,
Frail as though compounded of air and light,
Fanned him with the wafers of her wings
And with her inaudible heartbeats stirred

The down upon his cheek; He heard the incessant
Crackle of a palmtree . . . this
Identifiable and clear sound . . . then He saw —
Burning in bright points to flame, as prayer
Burns upward, ending in delirium —
The marble apices on temple hill
Suddenly darken . . .
And the palace of Herod, diamonded,
Blaze for a moment and grow dim
As a jewel on which a heel is set.

Light moved, in infinite order streaming,
In shining numbers to the sea
That rocked like a trapeze of fire, light —
Beautiful upon eyeless reaches where only dolphins
Disport before . . . the peacock of the sun . . .
Turned from Judea, humped and creeping
Himward along her sands. Darkness hooded
Her erect and several heads; staunchless
Darkness flowed in on him and He felt

The sinking earth beneath him keel,
Three crosses turning like a wheel
And whirled betwixt their spinning bands
Two thieves that clutched with bleeding hands
And bleated at the sky,

Wherefrom the moon crawled sluggishly
To feast upon the three;
The moon was like a silver leech
He could not lift a hand to reach
And pluck from off his eye.
The blind that He had taught to see
Jigged upon the keeling ground;
As in a pale green mist He saw
Young hills veiled in lavender
And with an argent nimbus crowned
Pace before him solemnly,
Circle thrice and bend the knee
As the kine did on that night
As they stood in the sweet straw.

He felt the Roman soldiers tread
Upon his body, stretched apart,
A trestle between earth and heaven;
He gave them of his peace unriven,
The silver silence of his heart
He broke like a sweet fruit for them
Till each unknowingly was shriven.

But they, marking his lip quiver, caught a faint word or so
And mocked him to each other, saying, He hath forgiven us.
The linked hills flung back, forgiven us, and they, too,

23

Smelling in the tufted evening the wisps of broom upon
   their sides,
Rippled with a mellow and secret laughter.

Yet not all laughed, or with the lips only and for good fellow-
   ship;
And these, seeing blood trickle in the baked meat,
For that day and the next ate only grapes and a wild honey.
And to listening women his word was as a date pit
To be sloughed out of red mouths, not tasting of its bronze
   and iron,
That should swing in a great arc from east to west and smite
   horizons like a gong.

2.

Young Romans sauntered, delicately perfumed,
   With a fine insouciance up the stark way
   Toward the appointed spectacle that loomed
Athwart the adventitious path, whereon they
Anointed casually the April air,
And masked with nice semblance of satiety
The unfastidious ardor of their stare.

All the steep hill was murmurous; there came
Important men among the Jews and talked
Until lime-colored evening endlessly.
The little vapours of their breath that forked
In arrowy spirals darted at his head,
Now haloed in the setting sun that staved
Out from it in great spokes. The thwarted light,
Gushing from the embolus the crosshead made,
Downward in a bloodied fountain, sprayed
The upturned faces on the mount; they shed
More tears than they had need of as they craned —
Each burning eyehole in the mask of light
That pressed his face — to cup before it paled
Amid the golden bubble of the air,
His image in their sight and burn him there,
The arrogant gall-flower of their root,
In effigy for ever.
                                        Yet be sure
There were few workmen in the crowd that payed
Oblique obeisance to the workman's son.
They, arm and axehead functioning as one,
Hewing out of cedars the great masts of ships,
Or shaping trees in which the sap had ceased
To redden the grain, leaving the fine pores
Hollowed like reeds through which the light should blow

Into the dark piths, into the iron cores;
Till the clear form of beauty be released
To curve about the daylights in a bow . . .
Forever drawn . . . before some eastern gate —
And all the shining wood, articulate,
Uplift to light the paeans of its doors.

They—whose feet were narrow on the mountains,
Quarrying marble for the shining town,
Slipping on the steep sides, with puny pull
Of bone and sinew dragging mountains down,
Subdued, to a king's feet; (such men as these,
With anonymous fingers beautiful
On the gates they might not enter in,
Upreared the pilasters of Megaron)
They — greatly fingering great stones, those keys
From which there should ascend high harmonies
To mount in lucent marble to the sky,
Or rise about the cities in a wall
Not all inflowing sands should cover quite,
But leave some snatch of stone upon the light
To show unborn centuries . . . with mass-psalms
Clangorous and terrible on their lips
Of stone and iron . . . the bondmen of this
Had song too in their hearts . . .

They, bent with straining sinews interlocked
In a vast cradle whereupon they rocked
The world securely, so not one bright drop
Of all her leaning goblets overflowed
To spill delight upon their lips, had little time,
(Whose dimmer dreams, aborted on each road
They builded, stirred and died without a cry)
To ponder him, or how his dreams had grown
To overgrowths within the temple bone
And spired, pulling their bright fabric down.

But moneychanger, Levite, publican,
Headmen from the slaves' quarters where they bred
Slaves in each other's arms, old men,
Creeping up the dusty buttocks of the hill,
With trays of many fruits, intent to sell
Ere holy Sabbath, here and there a woman,
Discreetly without ornament — all came
With various purpose, but a common aim —
To gain some sweet memento of his torment —
Some final reticence, folded about pain
That should be at the end stripped off — which they
Might seize and share between them . . . as the cerement
Of one who had proclaimed men equal — aye
Even unto slaves and women — and had pried

Open some ultimate wisdom like a fruit,
None might retain apart but all divide,
And babbled of some communal bright heaven.

Yet in the crowd —
Allied by privy purpose, in which all
Disparities of race, garb, color, all
That hues the chrysalis whereon light hovers,
And defalcation of its ray begins,
And differentiates each forkèd norm,
Assume like textures as do grains of skins,
When smoothed to parchment one writing covers —
There worked a darker ferment than all these.

An angle holding its clear sided form in the circle closing,
  Mary
Took the difficult path. Tears flowing through the long night
Had washed away the violet markings of her eyes, staring one
  way;
At the arcs, diminished to points in the blue irises, there swam
  minute,
Yet complete unto each curve of agony, the gleaming figure
  on the cross.
She did not see the small thick man, head round as a mush-
  room, mouth thrust forward,

Till his hot fingers closed upon her arm. Dost thou weep for
  him? he said. Mary
Looking down into eyes, the color of marshwater, the lustrous
  peripheries still, but the deeps
Quick with a secret motion, felt her exposed heart quiver, it
  is the beginning . . .
Why should I weep for him? He who this night shall be
  honoured of the angels.
It is for myself I weep, she answered, smiling from old habit,
  but her eyes
That beat like two blue wings about the cross, disdained
  him.
Thou shouldst not gaze on him, so long, made fast against
  that light. There is no light, she said,
But her heart screamed, O let there be no light! Pluck out thy
  jewel from its azure, God,
And hide it from all sight and let it burn . . . a secret diamond
  in thy breast. He said,
Thy grief hath made thee mad! mine eyes behold the sun there
  fairly vomiting with light.
Then let my darkness shine for thee; she would have pulled
  away her arm but he stammered,
Clinging, I am a stone-cutter; a man from Joppa — my name
  is — She did not listen,
Yet relaxing under his touch, finding it vaguely comforting.

29

The little blunt pebbles of his words, falling in her ear as
    through an open hand,
Even lulled her till she heard, It is the perfect moment, picked
    of his fine cunning —
What is it thou sayest? Nay, believe me, I too feel his nails —
    I —
Your words no more hold content of your heart than — An
    old courtesy held back the name
That yet grazed him with an invisible point. He noted
For the first time hollows in her throat, yet beautifully pillar-
    ing
From the bluish basins of its bone, and broke into a spurious
    laughter.
Thou laughest easily for one who feeleth nails that are not in
    his palms.
But in my soul, he said, and not to be plucked out, and
    Mary,
Who had seen desire in the faces of many men, but rarely
    that which she could not fill,
Beheld, in the shining strangers of his eyes, of the color of
    still water, coiling
With a secret and perpetual motion, some hunger that she
    could not quite
Identify; till, of those black deposits old days had left in her,
    there flared

A moment when she had lain, rabid and foaming on the earth
and seen

Between her and the sky a face. She said, I saw thee on a day
in Magdala, but he, blank-eyed:

I know not Magdala, then smirked, a goodly town, I've heard,
with comely

Women and kind. Thou fool, she said, again tried to shake
him off, but he cried,

I have a thing to say — a story will interest thee. I knew once
a young man

Who jumped from off a cliff into the sea — a great high cliff
. . . ee-e-e hadst thou but seen

The waters fairly boil there! — Why did he jump from off the
cliff?

He did not find some things the way men said they would be
or he thought they would be

When he came, a stranger into Joppa . . . he was a crazed
man talking . . . but he had an eye,

Like his there, with a flame in it. It was a comely day . . .
the town made holiday . . .

He was a fool, she said, to make your holiday. Wind, blowing
out her robe, spread her odor

Like a warm stain on the air. And he, thrust from her
borders, feeling invisible areas of her suddenly hostile,
babbled,

31

But I have not finished . . . there is something more . . . I
    am ashamed you should think there should be
Nothing more — As a trampled fire begins again to glow
A flame grew in the drowned eyes and before their too near
    blaze
That which worked overtly in his own, sank down from out
    the light.
Feeling an old fear chatter in him, he let go her arm, and Mary,
Released from the warm touch upon her flesh, as passive in
    their strife
As the slow-breathing earth to the wild traffic on her hill,
Turned on him in fury, Thou weevil in the ear, thou populous
    sick worm!
I will call upon the captain of the guard, I will tell him —
But the man from Joppa slunk into the crowd.

Mishael, small merchant of the market place, munching on a
    fig, meditatively
Waggled his black beard. His eyes, luminous and alert, pools
    of ink and a fly
Crawling . . . crawling . . . with inattention, as a weary
    man leans pack upon a stone,
Rested on the cross the litter of his thought. He was think-
    ing, perhaps,
Of his perfumes lost on the road from Damascus, when the
    camel

Shook itself . . . and the driver, fathered by a jackal, doz-
ing . . .

Or of his lastborn — harp-gold hair, benign blue eyes, smiling with the gentle

Condescension of the angels when they flew through the
cedars of Lebanon — who

Liked to sit in gutters after rain, pouring slime on her bright
hair . . . Mary

Wished to tear at the smooth beard, the wide mouth champ-
ing, see complacency

Change into amaze, amaze to fear . . . measured her distance . . . I am too tired . . .

She heard the chattering of the scribes, one to the other; ye
less than a rushlight,

That passing from hand to hand, scorcheth the last finger,
there is here a flame shall out-bide you all.

She looked on him with pride; then her eyes, clearing of the
teardrift, saw him plain:

Desolate and stark flesh . . . curling about the nailheads . . .
flies

About the withered garden of the mouth . . . only the eyes,
burning yet supreme,

Putting his will upon her and hasping it with a look . . .
He . . .

Dangled before these figurines . . . that earth

Might vomit over . . . or the super-stone crush without
    animus.   She turned,
Burying her eyes in the crowd as in muddied waters, and
    there
Beheld John with Mary the mother on his arm,
And observing thus these two
In tremulous communion making three with him they looked
    upon, she,
Who had born no man-god to the world, felt arise in her a
    dim hate
That, like a face uplifted from a bier to affright a lone watcher
    and sink down, died as it flared . . .
And she moved toward them with gladness as to his beloved.
But the mother, putting back her veil that she might the better
    see, and beholding
Between her and the cross that bright rapacious head, said
    softly unto John,
How wildly she doth look, and he, who would not look so
    upon such a day; but the old Mary,
There was that on the blue tip of her glance . . . grazed me
    as it leapt away . . .
I have never liked those eyes she burns against, like a woman
    sitting naked at her window . . .
The wind caught up the low uttered words and cast them like
    a larger sand

34

Out of its dry throat into the young haggard face, that wavered
  as a thing caught between two winds,
Then the bright head like a parrot's lifted and went on alone.

Three years ago this spring time, Mother Mary said to John,
He was at home with me . . . before the olives darkened . . .
He had gone.
Thou shouldst have seen him then — legs like two pillars of
  the temple. He hath lost much flesh
Since the last wine-treading. Had he come home to me, I
  had well cared for, I had fed him
Goats' milk from the pails at morning when it is rich and
  sweet with the good juice
Night brews in the dark bellies . . . but He . . . would not
  come home.
John did not answer; he whose quiet was as a shield pressed
  down hard upon a flame
Pondered this calm that flowed out from her, surrounding
  her,
He felt himself drawn as by a slow suction into its stilly
  waters
So that he too felt islanded, cut off from all this violent life
  beating upon them.
His face had a blurred look, as though long nearness to a
  flame had melted the fine lineaments.

35

His eyes were not identical;   one sheared astray from the
straight pure bevel of his glance;
Yet to be sure of this one had to look again.   She at his side
moved with a peasant majesty.
Her eyes were deep depositaries, bedding
Old wisdoms of the loam and its unending patience and all
green abiding habits of the earth —
Save there were no expectancies, merely old pain, might have
been sharp once . . . now
Worn down by long acceptance had no edge.   Her feet held
earth with certitude,
As sure of their estate;   she stood erect as a date palm, her
broad-leafed hand,
Made for large hospitalities, felt of her great breasts that
hung
Low unto her girdle, and pressed them secretly as though
she
Sensed in their deep reservoirs working an old sap
That soon should issue, taking the old way . . .
And He, too, seemed to gaze upon her there,
Hemmed in the shadow of their hostile heads,
As though He saw, traversing the blue day,
The very substance of her blood and bone
Outravel from her teats in two white threads
That played two streams of music on the air.

The crowd
Now teetering on its toes that they might the better see him,
Swayed as to the music of invisible pipes.

Mary

Resisting multiple invasion of arms, breast, thighs, nestled
    to the wind, tepidly coiling about her.
She longed for an arm, the comfort of a touch, needing her,
    that she needed.   Once
She met the gaze of a man she had slept with, but he — startled
    to recognition
Of that in her desperate and candent stare, promising no joy,
    turned back on her
An epithet of hate rose up in her dry throat and striving
With the inertia of her pain, sank back in her like a stone . . .
    she too
Wished to sink into some cool pit of darkness, drawing night
    down in her . . . primordial
Night, chaste, unknowing any pierce of light that applies
    bright torsions to those deeps
That long but to be still . . . O fingers of Ishtar, rest now
    on his fingers, casing fire . . .
O firm cool touch leaving torment in its wake . . . as though
    marble should be pithed with flame . . .
Old men of the Sanhedrin, jerked to a stiff sprightliness, as
    though

37

A senile April prickled in their parts, Syrians, Greeks, Jews

From Alexandria, Chios, Rome, come unto the feast of Passover,

Jostled her as they passed. Some turned to look back at the
gaudy head, but most

Sought but for vantage at the spectacle that should set this
day bannered and apart

And festoon their memories of this white walled town.

But there were some, out of Jerusalem, observing things. A
gangling

Youth with a sharp meager face, eye acrid as a quince, in-
drawn

Mouth like the slit in a tin flute, was first to cry on him.

At the pebble of his word, skating on its taut mood, the mob

Became a vast ribald mouth, uttering raging noises. Mary

Turning on him who had made the first jibe, cried in a harsh
high voice like a desert bird's,

He shall arise — ye shall be as palms under his feet — He shall
confound you utterly!

Hearing which some said, she is of his women — let us tell
the soldiers;

But others, seeing she was still young, with that in her eye
whereof they knew,

Guffawed loudly, and one, He hath the nose of a good honey-
beater, this Jew,

At which his fellows laughed the more, and they were of a
   pleasant humour, till a hand
Zigzagged toward her, wavered and then rallied, snatching
   feebly at her robe.   She struck;
It recoiled with precipitation, but in its place a dozen
Hands — not hesitant now or stretched of impure purpose, but
   with the righteous
Certainty of the group-errant — strove for hands, hair, gown,
   but she,
Shaped to the superior swiftness of things long hunted,
Slid from out their hold, in a moment was forgotten.   The
   mob
Oscillated, foaming along its crest, vociferating
Mouths spat out a fine spray, eyes, as with some fierce pressure
   from within
Crushing the fine membrane, always the mass surged,
As though straining for some ghastly equilibrium,
Inward about the cross, there — halted by the spears and the
   sprawling
Bodies of the soldiers — became a drove, docile, bewilderedly
   piling one upon the other —
Needing but a word, defining that which yet moved symbolless
   in the dark body —
To charge again, even upon spears.   Mary, wedged between
   its raving units,

Working, as with a maniacal desire for closeness,

Like grain upon grain of sand some force was pressing into
stone,

Met again the eyes of Mishael, not gentle now but focused on
some dim desire —

Not for his Hanna, who had borne him thirteen, nor for his
lost

Perfumes, nor for any sin of which he had heard or read . . .

She looked in the eyes of women, eyes pleasuredly chanting,
not my

Husband, lover, son, yet here, too, an alien wholeness . . .
women

Did not need this cardinal on white design, furrowing the
sunset . . . women

Spun whirled, not whirling, in the male dance . . . turning
. . . the hill is turning . . . God,

Send down thy chariots! Her hands clawed with a rending
motion at the sky,

Serene, softly ebullient, an immense blurred harmony

In which all things blended or were made solvent, one dark
note weaving

Endlessly in tireless circles, bearing without break the clear
theme . . .

She turned, struck madly at the swirling faces, eyelids

Flickered with a vague irritation, undeflected

Stares not turning her way, hands brushed away her hands
as one brushes away flies.
The tide of heads, necks craning in a single neck,
Bobbed, sank, rose again, stringently humming heads on
heads
Light coiled in them like a thread, unravelling, leaping to
fusions . . .
Light . . . burning to obscene revelation . . .
Floating over the mass in an envelope of fire not yet struck
to flame . . . O God
Let loose Thy lions, Thy rams straining beyond the gate!
From the matrix of the black cloud back of his head,
A beam played on his breast, glancing from his breast slant-
wise in the crowd,
Into the dirt, lice, stench, by way of the shining and clean
place . . .
Something wavered in her sight, not frangible, like a strong
web cleaving
To the crowd-shape . . . she thrust in it her hand . . . no
substance . . . announce Thyself beloved . . . the Face
Was moulded with a flagrant grace, the mouth
Like the mouth of a mask curled back and up; the attra-
hent
Eyes, in which desire was naked and unashamed as a child's
cry,

Burned with a terrible innocence, a corruption like the rot of
    light . . .
And when He . . .
Not now inert but erect with lifted head, etched as in a livid
    lightning
That swam in blazing colors as she stared, looked upon them
The eyes bayed.
Jerusalem
Shall have no heal in her but fire and devastation,
She shall burn with a great heat
And the waters of her eyes be as boiling springs . . .
Her light shall be visible unto Orion . . .
The stars in their shining multitudes shall gaze
Down on her with a long look . . . Jerusalem
Shall suspire green flames . . .
Corianders shall blow out of her wide doors . . .
The thrust of narcissus
Shall put floors asunder.

3.

On the taut string He was the night bowed somberly
     its ancient music;
     And He, attuned to diapasons,
Heard in the conch shell of darkness the murmur of many
     peoples.
Inevitably, crowds had sought him, without thought as they
     functioned, turning to him as to mate or eat;
Always, in their eyes, beyond the pleas for succor or surcease
     or for the celestial valleys,
The desire for some delirious intimacy; always He had fled
     from crowds,
Over sands, upon waters, into caves . . . but to return, put-
     ting his will upon them;
Now for him the love chase ended, that for them was at the
     dark beginning.
How should they have endured that ray of an inhuman clarity
     the desert
Gives to her communicants; those who, in that Light of which
     they are the violent shadows,
Grow bladed and of the fiber of lightning: he who beholds
After what arduous windings and lone watches —
The arcanum of light, coring all things —
Must not seek to lead men by a straight path unto its bright
     edge.

43

He who would lead men must see with them or beyond only a
little way.   Not all,
Even of the importunate, shall be admitted to the cabalas
of the light,
Who knoweth not this shall not see beyond it by that
farther ray,
He, whom the god-breath blew through, held there in him as a
reed holds song.
What matter, before the incendiary spark, driving to inevi-
table impact,
The long or short road to one end: there shall remain,
thumb-printed on the quarried stone,
Splintered of the mountains, things done this day in Judea, now
No more than a fleck of ash on the pomegranate of the sunset.

He felt strange fluxions in him and tender and sharp vibra-
tions;
Mob cries, the kisses of the whip that were as mouths pressed
too close;   the faltered
Kiss of Judas, faintly malodorous like a jonquil that had lain
too long on the breast of a dead man,
Chill yet on his cheek;   the warm kiss of Mary and pressure
of John's bright head
All blent in a vast music not again
To sound apart in any separate strain,

44

But move in the clear whole wherein He whirled
Incandescent, in the pillared flame
Of music that is time made audible
With all its massed formations high in air
And wheeling columns streaming out of sight —
To what bright conquest or achieved despair
Or flaming end past compass or compute —
Music, over time made absolute,
Holding eternal, in the light that moves
From sun to sun an octave in its flight,
The little hatreds and the chiming loves.

He in lone days in the desert had known
Strange songs of passage, on those desolate airs,
That rested in their flight on him who sat
So still there in the silence, listening,
The sands o'erflowed the arches of his feet
They all but covered as they cover stone.
And He, under the immense shadows pressing
A strange bright torsion on his soul, had fed
Them honey of his heart and snared some few
That He might share their music with his people.
Yet when He strove — hearing all dissonant
Voices and unpremeditated notes
In one vast choral blending — to intone

45

A clear strain of the profuse harmony,
Some string, no more responsive to his touch,
Hung thawn and twanging without music. Now
Bereft of the winged blood that once had borne
The song to glamorous ascension, He
Heard the supreme moment pass . . .

Strange things grew in the night — as in a vast April moving
    on the void,
And monstrously flowered. From unknown territories,
    jungle and primal loam,
Unnameable resurrections, ungainly and gross signs life at
    heat
Made out of her first slime, watched him with small fierce
    eyes, asking a dim question
Flowers He had seen no like of nor colors to surpass their
    shining
Beat about his face like dragonflies about a flame, and there,
Drifting in the current of his breath, went out like lights.
And when He for their bright sakes would have put forth
    warding hands,
A birdfoot rested on each palm and would not be denied . . .

Pain died in him in heaps; He lay
Watching the strange figures night dandled in her soft dark
    hands; yet heeding under all

The far-off mutter of the desert, licking her dry parts . . .
    her sands
Lolling in the darkness . . . tufts of grass on the bare hills
    . . . the stretched
Sinews between mountains, bowelled with iron . . . He missed
    no least vibration
Of the savage beautiful body or cadence of its organic music.
Strange figures circled him, stark trees that bore strange carv-
    ings on their boles, inhuman
Over growths of form and face, whereof each driven line —
    running in a fierce stopless sweep as though the hand
That ploughed the stubborn wood had reached out anguished
    from a flame —
Seemed dedicate to some appalling purpose. Here was that to
    which was no appeal;
No weakness, wheedling the shut heart to cherish or retrieve
    from the bright holocaust
Beloved thing. As each stalked by it could be said the mask
    moved . . . there was a perceptible
Motion of the large lips, drawn back in a vast snarl shaping,
    It is He. In the cavernous
Eyeholes, lit by a dull glow as of fires that had fiercely burned,
    yet smouldering, He discerned
As across infinite spaces, confused figures, but whether of
    man or beast

Or what they darkly wrought He could not see . . . yet felt
in him an old horror rising.   These

Were suffused with a strange light not of the moon or sun nor
related to any star.

And He was amazed before them as to see mountains walking.

The night was coruscant with eyes

Eyes that seemed to float detached and faceless, eyes of lions
and of wolves, carnelian

Eyes glowing in great masks of wood and stone, glimmered
with obscure intent

There was a terrible familiarity in those eyes, demanding that
which He could not give.

Presuming in him a dim knowledge which He did not
share.

He felt troubled there should be some thing which He could
not give, or any veil

Between him and the darker fire . . . It was in a topaz
eye

Wheeling in narrowing circles, at the nave, contracting and
expanding in corona of fire,

He perceived at last naked as in lightning, that which spired
at the core

Of the peripheries blazing . . . and darkness

Welled up like a black fluid in his throat, and all his spirit
retched in him.

48

Stars . . . glimmering in compact points profound and afar
off . . .

Light grew in him like a stalk . . . up and up . . . to meet
the far shining . . .

As it was at the beginning . . . the first stammering upon the
waters . . .

In his heart, now at an end of strife, having fed into the pure
stream

Of purpose even the undefiled hopes yet in the dark pod, a
pellucid

Junction, as of that which had been severed again whole and
without seam.

Earth . . . watching out of her seas, great eyes lidded in
darkness, sluggishly lifting

The night that drooped upon them . . . slip and pull of
tides, under the fragile

Fingers of the moon . . . dark flesh of evening glowing
under the moon . . .

Muscles of the rivers supplely gliding . . . earth supine

In the vast equations of the night that upbore her as on immense wings . . .

He expanded, treading upon space, through him sweetly
flowing

The effluvia in which all things move. He heard

Out of the unfathomable arches and stretches of the night

The moments falling. Summers endlessly uncoiling from off the golden

Spool of the sun and dawns like bare-foot virgins with the early wonder in their eyes

Re-passing in silvery procession; He attuned

To all delicate sounds of things and their infinite textures, knowing

Trees by the differing cadences of leaves that prattle to the ear

Sweetly of no thing . . . and of the vanity of a rose . . . and how stone

Cries at the emergence of great waters while yet these

Are but a bubble of silver on the cave's lip.

He who, on days when all things fasted from the light, while earth

Contorted as with a vast madness, gathered

Her sands to fling at the sun's face, had heard

The heartbeats of flowers and tremors along the nerves of leaves,

Heard now the feet of centuries . . . in these

Enormous footfalls all other sounds were lost. It was a silent world.

Until into its silence that was as the heart of song or as the quiet at the core of hurricanes,

A word out-leapt, an overgrowth
A bloody hand, shaped like his own,
To a separate life from out his mouth.
(The wind blew salt in each nail-hole
It fanned into a living coal)

In vast semi-circle thrown
Sleeping lay the curved horizon,
Till the hand that spanned the zone,
The streaming hand shaped like his own,
Seized and swung it like a scythe.
He saw the spinning blade divide
The ancient body of the night,
A humming scimitar it cleft
The blue deep parts within her nave
No other vaulting thing had reft
And plunged in some high fountain-head
That trumpeted with light,
And spurted on the void and dripped —
As stark against the sky He swung —
As freshly hot as from a heart
Its burning solace on his tongue.

Light gushed out of the rift and made
A radiance upon the mountains,

Light supernal, turning the rocks to fire,
Holding the seas before it like a glass
Compelling to its own fabulous desire
The small pure waters of his sight
So that for a moment the Omnipotent,
Blazoning his face above the mountains,
Might look therein and be made glad;

Light, from his eyeballs raying
As when a vessel is filled too full
Light, focusing on such things
As a nude girl or a goat or a white bull
It made burn with unsupportable luster.
Light, over his senses playing
Streaming out of the facets of the cross, whereon
He stemmed out taut as a white flag
Light, blazing a wide path to Rome as to the heart of a poppy
    seed.

Light omnivorous and without mercy
Consuming all things for fuel —
Denying no toad beast man fowl worm,
Seizing, transfixing the mean norm,
Leaving it starrily, as it left Peter
Pierced with the white crow of dawn

In the arrested moment, like a spear,
To remain without falling and without flight,
A cynosure to burn forever there
Impaled on the implacable light.

Light making bright things its own,
Implicit in it all dark gestations
Of life that terribly flowers and burns again to the white
    bone;
Light, no god might blow on with his jealous breath
Nor the chained mountains stamp on with a ponderous foot,
Informing the night's arteries, swelling the great hill-roots,
Down,
Full veins of earth, purpling the dim strata,
Down
Through the dark declivities, touching the riant fire under the
    world . . .

Until his spirit, merging into the light's excess,
Grew one with that which fed on it . . .
Light, falling on Judea, smiting her rocks to song . . .
O Hills, tearing at your nailed feet, you too singing . . .
All things resolving into light and light in love . . . denying
    no toad beast man fowl worm . . .
In one song of monstrous adoration.

53

He crushed the night like a blue grape
In his clenched spirit; thirstily
He drank deep of the heady brew
Of purple juice that ebbed from it.
Through emptied arteries he drew
A dark transfusion in each vein,

Till loosed in a submerging flood
The bloodied waters of his brain
Flowed in on him and a cry
Hurtled from his lips,
A cry that was the light's eclipse
And pealed against the desolate sky,
Making a gray void in space
Of the bright thing He was,
Spreading on the day oblivion
And darkness where a flame had shone.

Earth
Swung to a full period
And all her reeling mountains stood.

He, whom the bowing hills adored
Impaled them there upon his word;
It poniarded the hills like flame;
They stood transfixed as by a sword;

The ground sank humbled to its place,
And at the feet that Mary loved
Lay sullen as a beast reproved.

The little wind that licked his face
Was the only thing that moved . . .
The little wind that hushed itself
And crept down to the sea
And dawn as white as Mary came
On the horizon, strangerly.

Earth quaffed the morning pure and cold
As a long drink.   But his black drouth
Was not eased by the dew that turned
Into a dandelion gold
The glistening hairs about the mouth
From which the singing flame had burned.
When the east was rosy as a grape
Before it purples, and alone
Venus, on the milky nape
Of morning, slavered by the sea,
Glimmered like a precious stone
There gaped, in darkness, emptily
The blackened scabbard of his mouth
That held a blessing's shape.

55

II
JOHN

Swiftly through the woods John sped away,
     Yet not so swiftly that he missed the spoor
     Of mating snakes, made in the April night
Just over, or the prints of furry feet.

In some serener ear within his ear —
That had it fathomed this day's agonhead
Had sent no haggard tidings for his blood
To carry to the little frantic heart
That beat a desperate drum in the still wood,
But closed upon it softly as the air
Closes on a cry, or as the sands that flowed
Like water in his steps — he overheard
The infinite murmur of the multitudes
That run out of their doors from a stone's eaves
Or from the old sanctuaries of bark
In the lightstream flowing crystal clear
And without color — frail things
That hold their tiny revels on a thorn
Or on the green spire of a reed and pass
In some bright avalanche of dew that slides
In thunder from a flower of grass.

In him fire-footed chills
    Prickling with an icy heat
Crept like many centipedes
    Crawling on a thousand feet.

But in the suave and pliant air
    Was no dark thing to eschew
Or rive with any bladed prayer.
    Milkily the morning blew

In through him as through a door
    That opened from within
And he felt the little wings of light
    Brush soft against his skin.

Morning came with innocence,
    Benign as dew upon His lip —
Who held the desert like a cloth
    On which the sacrifice should drip;

Morning, streaming like a dove,
    Touched with silvery diffidence
His two feet like flying fish,
    Cleaving shadows in their dance;

Morning perfect as a wish
  Forever unfulfilled; he smelled
Her tender cedar-scented flesh
  And robed in pallid radiance,

Vestal mornings fair as this,
  Appointed on the chosen Hill
To work the havoc of His will,
  Came silverly through memory,

And, shining with a threefold light,
  Gleamed in him as diamonds might,
When shaken from the jewelled fist
  Of the bright disturbèd dust.

Dawns with lustrum on their brims
  Bore the light as in a vase,
Nor spilled one incandescent drop
  To set His lovely world ablaze,

Nor broke light's vagrant promises,
  To every frail thing that moves
And bears the anguish of its loves
  And walks alone,

To scorch no least audacious wing
 In its bright circle hovering
Too fondly near; dawns jasmine
 That held the light as in a cup.

He, who these several springs had moved
Beside him whom he loved
In sweet accord,
As of two puissant young wings that bore
One body in its flight,
Knew this spot well.
Here the scarlet lilies threw
Their bright invulnerable seed
To any wind — some said they fell
From out the piercèd side of one
Who died upon an ancient hill
And left a singing in men's blood
As in the grass, an old refrain,
Not all the years had quieted,
That yet sang on — here He had paced —
Feeling the need of loneliness that John
No more invaded than a tree or stone.

Here — following thy head that ever reared
Too early from its stone or wisp of straw,

In dawns with that strange stillness in the air
That comes up before thunder — I have heard,
In these dim cedars, clashings as of bright
Accoutrements of angels, flying near,
Who caught upon high boughs imperilled hair,
That tore upon the wind
Or on a sudden bird
Or on a sharp angle of the light.
O I have seen them, in their serried flight
Strew an alien luster on the air,
Made darker for their brightness, and then pass . . .
Leaving a glamor on the common day
And in my heart a shining . . . yet have never
Dared to tell thee lest thou smile
In that intolerant sweet way of thine.

There is a quiet in this place that is not peace —
Thou didst not come here for peace . . .
O Lord, leave me these moments . . . do not pace
Forever by me on this path.
Why shouldst thou stoop to slay me with a smile?
O gaze at me in wrath
So I may cherish thy changed looks and bear
A stranger image in my heart
Of a strange man who died this day and was not thee.

When thine eyes put hand upon his sword, his face dissolved
    like an old moon . . .
The faces there about thee circling
Went out like blown bubbles one by one.
It seemed the very stars had disappeared
Leaving thee isolate . . .
A soldier stumbled . . .
The night grew mutinous with feet.

Judas . . . sandling through the torches . . . Judas
Thy singing breath blew in
His spirit, stopped up like a flute
That hath no opening; thy silver note
That could not issue from his different throat
Stuck in his hollow heart and made therein
Discordant music thou couldst not confute.

Yet I have seen wild music, in his eyes,
Blocked of its natural passage, gleaming there
In tips of horned fire . . . and die down
Leaving a corpselight burning . . . I have known
There such a piteous knowledge and amaze
As it was shame to look on and not cover
Decently and tiptoe from the bleak place, where love
With hate died in embrace and left their blowth
For this day's livid flowering.

I always felt there was a strange dark man,
Among us, whom I did not know . . . Last night
He seemed a maggot thick, standing there bared
Of all wherein he had well wrapped himself
To throw a larger shadow on the light
Than had been his to throw. It was not pelf
Nor pride . . . nor that he could not sing . . .
It was some other and some darker thing
That goaded him, and that he had not shared
With thee or any other soul he loved —
If he did love one, even thee —; he moved
Amid the multitude of the olive trees,
That seemed to lean all one way like a crowd
Craning toward some bright spectacle, as though he
Were but the shadow of a cindered tree,
The burning forests of thine eyes had snared
As tinder for the common flame, and now
Had no more substance, save in memory.
There was a shuffling sorrow on his brow;
His eyes were fixed before him on one spot
And did not rove . . . as though his gaze had caught
On some thing there he saw and we did not.

Mary's: Thistle-head, go blow upon the wind — thy gold
Hath not been tried in fire . . . Mary

65

Came out of the jacinth evening soundlessly.
She smelled of cinnamon.   The stars
Burned on her forehead . . . and her little breasts
Glimmered through her raiment.   Did you not see
The men fall back as before spears?
They were not armed against her . . . she
Worked like leaven in their blood . . . the night
Was filled with her and leaned
Above us with her paining weight . . .

                                        And then
I was alone in all those quiet trees
Where nothing stirred within me but my heart
That faintly beat.   The pulse of evening slowed
To a dim rhythm mine no more outraced . . .
I lay down on the grass and lizards moved
With noiseless feet on me as on a stone.

Lord, I have known no woman . . . was it Mary
Pierced me with a word and thrust me through?
How else shouldst thou have thought I left thee . . . *she*
Had thy last look.

There is some menace in this place
So still but now . . . the branches writhe
With obscene movements toward me . . . the white bones

Of fanged Jerusalem had been more kind
Than these stark treeboles circling . . . it seems
A presence walks with me that is not thine . . .
There is a madness in my mood . . . O Lord,
I need the comfort of thy touch . . . stand here,
Between me and those loopholes in the leaves,
That blaze with dreadful purpose! even light
Is tainted with some strange infection; dawn
Is like a mindless woman lying,
Too close against me, with her pallid mouth
That sucks upon my heart . . . blood . . . blood . . .
The world is one vast snout and roots for blood . . .
Ah, do not smile upon my fear . . .
Why must thou pierce me? I am calmer now.
Behold, I lift the light on my two hands
That do not tremble any more . . . but see
How hushed the morning lies upon my hands —
It is a still-born child I bear for thee
To breathe on and make live.

　　　　　　　　O thou art filled with ruth
Save for those hearts that cherish thee. Make manifest
Thy Majesty before the peoples. Come!
Armed with thy Father's lightning and beat
Upon this hollow world that is thy drum

Till it shall gape . . . and at their frantic feet
Burst like an old wineskin.

                  And thou shalt walk again
In that deep hush in which bright things are born,
And thou shalt sing, and I shall be thy horn
To sound thy golden tidings. I have known
Thee all my days.

               When the light stinging hail
Fell pure and without stain out of God's hand
That opened over the white storm, thy kiss
Blew faintly salt upon my cheek . . . O this
No doubt can shake nor any smile impugn!
At breastling day, companioned by gulls
And winds and piping waters, I have heard
Thy voice in their exultant trinady;
And when we paddled home with silvered hulls,
Wet-scaled and slippery, and sagging net
That dragged a load of stars along our wake,
And we sat hushed in the low pressing night
Running with dark wines that overflowed
The dim gold vase of evening, it was thee
I sought, eyes ranging the blue-tippled sea
Serried as with many helmets moving.
As moons that shine at daybreak and which dim

Eyes glimpse and lose amid the gaining light
Yet move on the horizon, silver-bowed,
In fadeless luster, hidden from the sight,
Thou wert a strange bright happening, remote
From vision, yet forever on its rim.
And yet thou camest softly, without blare
Of any gilded trumpet or aught other
Annunciation than the light that lay
With the usual glamour on our boat.

I do remember how the old blue sea
Shuffled in glistening coils about the day
That cast thy shadow on our street and how
From out the passing litters, in which bared
White jewelled arms moved languidly their fans
And topaz glimmered in the small pink ears
That curled about thy voice, shrewd eyes outstared
Outdiamonding the twinkle of the sands.
And shambling beggars, marketing their sores,
Peered from out their festered eyes, that bore
The riant light yet in them like a thorn,
With a dull wonder at thee, I recall
How gaping venders let the looting flies
Descend on the ripe figs . . . the while thine eyes,

That burned as though each amber disk had worn
Too thin before the dangerous light it veiled,
Glowed golden, sun-wise, equally on all.

These are the common memories young James
And I toss to and fro on rainy nights
As children throw bright stones up in their hands . . .
Of that which flowed from thee in through our souls
That echo faintly still, we may not speak.
How shall I put against thine ear a word
Should hold its uncontainable harmony,
Or, communicant again at the bright source,
Retrieve that moment in first purity

On which I was upborn or seemed to float
As sand in a great wind when light and sound
Sweep through its dancing particles; my heart
Swung outward pealing like a new-wrought bell
Over the steepening waters — if a bell
Can ache and tremble, knowing in its throat
The strange inrushing colors of the air
And their invading fragrances . . .

                                        And yet
'Twas James who bade me tarry when thou healed
The beggar's lip. James said this is the man

Whose feet I follow along many ways;
Whose voice exhorts me in my dreams; his breast
Is roomy as the sea's and warmer comforting;
His arms are wide as earth. The canker gleamed
A white blotch in the sun . . . the blue-gold day
That shone on it was unappalled, but I
Flinched in the hardy sunlight . . . and thy full
Lip curved on me in tender scorn; thine eyes
Pierced all my poor defences till I stood
Abased before their intolerant love.

Ah, this is why they hate thee . . . only blood
Can cool the searing fire of that glance
That tears apart the calyx without seam
And without blemish, starrily revealing —
Under the lustrous dust in the guarded
Darkness beyond the radiant pallor —
The desitude of the mean room. O Lord,
We are thy least vibrations and thy word
Hath made eternal all our little loves,
Transfigured now in the great light that moves —
From sun to sun an octave in its flight.

Thy hands are yet unpierced, thy feet
Are yet blemishless upon the green miles,

Only the wind of the white road hath kissed
Thy brow, there are no thorns amid thy hair . . .
The bugles of the light are blowing . . . now,
Even upon the elected hour, tear
This hill from out the earth's side
And send the cross timbers whirling.

Had I but faith . . . dear Lord, have I not faith?
O blow once more upon me with thy leavening breath:

Arise, dark hill!
Out of the dust and walk,
Nostril of the earth
Blow fire and smoke,
Vomit thy rubies
And thy amethysts,
Descend, unbidden
Guest, upon their sabbath feasts —
Come, wearing thy diamonds!
Let the sleeping shepherds
See through their shut lids
The shadow of a mountain
Move against the sky
And the glamour of their burning —
Let the temple rock,
Belly of the earth

Spue fire and smoke!
There was no sound of hammers yet, nor any voice
Lifted in love or turpitude. Dim earth
Impassive, unawaiting any backward look
Of him, whose unassembled dust she swirled
In some forgotten dance, yet darkly curled
Slept stonily along her quiet miles.
He felt a breeze stir
The shining thicket of his hair
That held no thorns for the smooth brow,
And gazing on his changeling hands, that drew
The almond pallor of the light,
Compared them curiously, as one
Amazed to see them scathless yet and fair.

III
JUDAS

I.

The sky had a clear pallor and the moon
Was large above the field which seemed to float
In luminous opacity, a square
Of moonlight, hearted by a tree
Ensconcèd in the lilac mist, a shape
That stirred upon the moonlight sluggishly
And drew light inward through a thousand leaves
Down and in unto the lusting core.
The shimmering faces of the lilies swayed
A trifle in the reeds — there was a wind —
As Judas came in softly through the gate
That was the final goal of the blind path
It ended. Once out of the dimmer wood
He seemed to hesitate; amazed that light
Should be in clear possession of this place
He had so long held tenure of in thought.
His hand closed on a thistle and he pressed
His foot hard down upon a stone, as though
To force avowal from the plant and stone
Of their subservience to the mastery
Of foot and hand; then mumbled in his beard
And, squatting on the earth, from out the palm
Had borne upon the thistle plucked out thorns

Sch, sch! they may be listening — they ran all ways; who
knows but they have followed us.
John's legs are like a stag-hound's and as swift—
That tree-bole might well hide the narrow withe he is.
Well, well? Why dost thou look at me askance, thine eyes
accusing
Me of that thing that thou didst instigate — didst thou not
say unto me, go to,
Thou art not man nor hawk but snail-spoor on the grass,
dove's dropping on a leaf,
And thou wilt serve men who despise thee. Up Judas, be a
man — make those who love not fear thee —
Didst thou not speak so Mary?
He said this night one of you shall betray me . . . I had
finished my lamb but Matthew
Choked on a morsel, Matthew is a slow eater. I said Master,
is it I? Peter sat up;
His gray hair bristled like a broom that is set upon the dust;
All moved as under a sudden torsion, the fair head of John,
Like a dandelion a scythe drops among the sheaves,
Sank forward on his breast. I said Master, is it I, and a blade
of light
Shone naked between us as though 'twere a sword and for
the swifter hand.
I stood and looked down at him where He sat, staring at the sun

78

That was a great hoop of gold on the horizon. I knew the sun
Streaming out from my head as with a radiant intention,
Would dazzle John if not He; his desert eyes looked the sun
    in the face,
His skin was suffused with a golden pallor; He was yet
    fragrant of the nard —
The price of which had filled an hundred of his poor ill-
    smelling.
I said Master, is it I, meeting his impassable look with a secret
    and jovial smile.
At last we knew each other and I . . . the thing I had to do
Which I had felt move in me many days, each day waxing
    larger, till my spirit
Grew heavy as a beast in foal with the dark weight of it.
Wouldst thou believe it had taken his word to free me? Even
    then
Had one but said, as I went out the door, Whither goest thou,
    Judas, or tarry with us yet . . .

He was not a leader, Judea
Hath lost no leader in him, He
Was not the man to take her out of bondage.
Until that day we entered in Jerusalem — I trudging at his
    ass's tail,
That threshing upon flies did spite me oftener than a fly —

79

I had not known him in a multitude

Weaving in and out among them like a thread

On which they moved in unison. It was a mood

He could not have kept up; I know this now, He danced
  too swift to take

A multitude for partner. Yet on that day

He rode his ass as it had been a war-horse. The young girls
  threw palms . . .

His eyes did not attest one palm, or lift it with a look — was
  that the way

To act before the people? I said unto the people

Think ye He shall lead ye to pleasant vinyards — Not even
  to a lean field

With a few poor wheat ears and a showing of corn — would
  ye follow a mad goat, I said,

It headed for the bare hills — would ye your eyes became
  apples for the vultures?

An ye follow me, I said, ye shall wear good linen and drink
  fine wine,

Ye shall loll in chariots . . . Mary, little pigeon, did not I
  speak so unto the people?

Do not tell me I did not speak thus to them. It is the way of
  a woman,

A man talks and talks and she, head-feather of a wagtail, does
  not listen!

But what to do now . . . advise me, little dove — canst thou
  not speak who wast so glib this eve
As I lagged by the way; didst thou not say then, Go —
Fulfill thy bargain! Hadst thou advised me — while there
  was time, the silver
Yet in their coffers, light, dusting with a golden pollen the
  black rose of earth,
He sitting in the inn — for they would talk interminably,
  the lamb-bones yet on the table —
Hadst thou then whispered in mine ear, withold, restrain
  thyself . . .
Well, well, shall we go home — the first thorn bush, cactus
  for a pillow.
The night boiled blackly in his eyes that stared down at the
  young grass;
Why did I give up all to walk in this man's footsteps in which
  mine were lost?
It was that I was sad, all parts of me infertile, my ways parchèd
  . . . and his soul,
Flowing on those about it as the Nile
Inundates the dry lands, made all
My waste to blossom as a meadow. Then his light waned
  and the dark solstice
Of his dream came on. My soul went lame with treading in
  his ways

That steepened to our feet, he taking all for granted — I
Might better have been beggar on the road for his attention. Ere that time
None questioned Judas' stewardship of his gold; none was uncivil: Andrew's
Was a still soul weaving, at home in its own twilight, like a woman's; none
Had heeded Andrew passing without word, and Peter was a kind man, Peter
Did smile on me sometimes
But James and Mark and Jude and Luke,
Those loud-mouthed brothers to all men, barely looked at me when they spoke.
I took much thought so they might have new bread, fresh meat and wine enough;
When John was foot-sore with much walking and could scarce
Set skinned heel on the ground, I brought him rice with honey . . . John
Turned from me as from a smell on the wind.
What did they want of me — that I put my body upon their dish?

He stared out darkly at the field, ensilvered
In the light that was its shining currency;

Dartles of silvery fire threaded
The air in continuous passage, silver
Trickled from the brimming cups of lilies
The wind pushed, and whitened on the tree,
Ashimmer as with a spurious flowering.
He held his hands up, catching the descending
Light that flowed down evenly in fevered
Palms that shook a little; he saw the still
White pool of silence oscillate, slip soundlessly
Back into the sea of light, observed
With what impartial glory it streamed down
Upon far domes as over the whispering
Congregation of the lilies:

                    He hath known
Little of silver, for all of his great lore,
Its courtesy to the touch, its sheen. Now I
Have the gift of silver as some men of tongues.
Show me an hundred coins, I shall pick one —
Hath been changed at the Fish Gate, from an old wife's
    pocket —
That is shot with changeling colors, which the sea
Hath shaken out of some galley, keeling
Head-down or washed up in a drowned sailor's pouch
Or a shekel of the temples dull as whore's eyes . . .

When He had given unto the innkeeper,
The bag on my arm felt light as a quail-feather —
                        Silver
                        is tractable and gentle;
                        it hath dawnsweet in it
                        and the savor of bitter waters;
                        it hath the eyelight of seagulls
                        and of the white peacock
                        and the indomitable gleam
                        of the eyes of the priestess
                        who pleasureth the stranger
                        and bestoweth herself without joy,
                        holding her soul aloof,
                        for gold is for harlotry but silver
                        is the virginity of the heart
                        and cannot be taken away —

Before the flying pieces of their silver
The sleeves of the money-changers flapped like fins;
Their wide mouths opened and shut without noise. When
  he scattered the silver
I knew then we served different gods . . I said unto them
That which He hath done unto your silver, that will He do
  unto you —
Of you too will He make sweepings to be borne off by the
  slaves at morning.

Thou wilt bear witness, Mary, I spoke so unto the money-
  changers.

                    Silver hath a flower
                    of a mellifluous brightness
                    that blossometh by night
                    on the pillows of the lonely —
Thou babbleth of a silver solvent as moonlight,
I would have that which I may grasp and hold —
                    it is an eater of light
                    and consumeth without return,
                    it is chaste and austere
                    and more glamorous than death
                    when washed and made fair
                    for beloved eyes —
Why dost though speak so soft Mary, thy voice was loud
  enough once.
I used to fear that He would hear thee — He
Who heard flowers tremble when a bee droned by —
And thou babbling, at midnight, like a brook
This moon will be five moons that thou hast lived in me,
Moved in the byways of my body, sat
With me in the blue twilight, listening
To their loud hopeful chatter by road sides
Or at inn-fires, and at night
Watched through the curtain of my spirit, stars,
Or if I slept plagued me with dreams . . I well

Remember the first day on which thou camest;
'Twas on the dusk of Friday and the paschal
Lamb was on the table and the steaming rice.
I heard thee speak in thy sweet usual tone
And all but dropped the dish John passed to me
With vague aversion in his glance.   Why dost thou hold
Thy body from me Mary — is it from fear
Of him who will not take and use it for himself?

Yet I have heard thee mock him and upbraid
Me for my fear of him and trembled, watching
The variable oval of his face,
Lest He surprise our secret.   Thinkest thou
He knew ought of it?   He is a jealous
God; all gods are jealous, even I . . .
Why dost thou smile and look at me askance —
Knowest thou not I am a god — hast thou not seen
My mother in this place and a dim glory
All about her head?   She walketh when the moon is large,
The way it is to-night, like a great burning
That hath come up, out of those hills,
Pushing apart the calyces of stone.
There is a teeming darkness in those hills
Bright things come out of . . . all the darkness, eyed,
Beholding above it and afar off

86

The proud intelligence of the perishing
Light . . . once, from the bottom of a deep pit
I saw stars by daylight . . . there is a darkness
For which shall be found no ray . . . long enough . . .
Come hither, little hawk, I will anoint thee
With such fire as the wings of moths
Sustain . . . and do not curl up in a crisp;
Make thee communicant at the bright fount —
Canst thou endure its shining — let fall into thine ear
A secret like a pearl: we three
Are the trinity of which He spake . . .

Slowly, as a cloth is drawn from off a bier
The lustrehead of silver faded from the lilies.
Beyond, in the transfiguring moonlight, stalks of stone
Flourished upon the dark and monstrously flowered;
Dim flights of domes ascended and were updrawn
Into measureless sapphire, pronged with stars,
From whose glittering boundaries, light
Streamed upon Jerusalem.

2.

She drifted softly, through the night,
Like a larger lily of the field
That danced and wavered in his sight
With all its grassy company.

Meek things that crept along the ground
Drew in their horns, a million spheres
Of dew broke with a silver sound,
Hairy rushes massed like spears
Broke in their lines and swayed apart
To close again, the lilies braced
Their narrow shoulders needlessly;
Not any tiny thing concealed
And trembling at a flower's heart
Suffered for her coming; she
Who leaned upon them did not brush
Away the lighted dust of pollen
From the bright hair of a stamen
Nor bended one helmet-headed rush.

Yet when he touched her as she lay
In light that was her only raiment
She seemed as heavy as a hill;
He could not raise her from the claimant
Earth that held her where she fell.

Mother, I know thee by the way
Thou pullest over thee the wet
Wild grasses like a coverlet;
I know thee by the few gold hairs
In the brown mole, there, near thy chin —
I know thee by thy little ears.
He threshed about her like a fin
With uncouth tenderness, but she
Lay still and did not look at him.

She might have been a wounded thing
Cast down from some high wall of space,
She lay with such beseeching grace,
One arm bent backward like a wing,
Motionless, and eyes upturned
To drink the fluent light, as one,
Born to the azure and having learned
To range the highways of the sun,
Can tread securely but on air.

When he lifted up her shining hair
That rippled in the night unbound;
It glided like a silver water
Through his fingers to the ground
He could not keep her buoyant hand

That was shapen like a morning prayer
Nor make it rest upon the ground.

She gave no word when he besought her
Nor glance; her blue evasive eye
Seemed hanging by a thread of light
That stemmed from a far path of sky
Where stars were thickest clustering . . .
Mother, he said, there is a thing
I cannot sleep on nor forget.
Put thy hand here and ease the strain
Of the string that pulls upon my brain.

As long ago when I did measure
Halfway and a half head over
To thy heart's indifference,
Twirl, O twirl, a moonbeam there,
Upon thy wrist, as though it were
A silver bangle for my pleasure —
As thou wert ever kind and strove
To pleasure that thou didst not love.

The moon, now supreme over those bare hills,
Traileth her bright hair upon the waters
We see not, yet are ever conscious of

And the wind tanged with salt blowing our way.
Let us arise, O mother, and go hence,
From out this arid place that is too far
Inland from the sea.   Shall not the moon
Bearing us silvery company, lighten
All ways that darkle at our feet?   O sly
And beautiful, whom I can no more move
Than I could lift a beam of this pale light
That lieth weightless on the lilies, come.
We shall behold the young day, radiant,
Dabble all bare and gleaming in the foam
Of the moon-swollen tides; the ivory
Breasted, the bridal-hearted, who bestoweth
Her favors upon all shall not deride
Us twain nor shall the sea deny, the sea
Who hushes with enormous lullabies
The heart that slows unto her pulse.   My soul
Hath become sick with looking on this thing
In which is less than two days' life . . . beyond
The span of a third sun dead meat shall smell
Unless they dress it with sweet unguents . . God —
Should I intrude upon his business?   He
Hath not torn up temples by their marble
Roots nor aimed at me his lightning: Behold
Do I not walk unscathed before his sight

Amid the shining traffic of this field
Where pass a trillion gossamer-winged things
About their minute business, unafraid?
Mother, there is a question in thine eyes
That drink the stars and will not turn on me
Their blue and frigid lustre —is it this
That thou wouldst know, why I did do this thing?
I tell thee, 'tis too costly to the self
To disentangle motives and to stare
Too long upon the stalk of life erect
Till sight turn inward and the eyes blur
And darken to find ultimately this
Hollow at the red pith of fire . . . there
To circle infinitely and never
Return unto the kind light.   Let us go
Down to the old sea whose profuse salt
Assoils those hearts too sullied for small streams
To wash their filth away.   We two shall share
Her large forgetfulness, we two shall walk
In innocence — and none shall know us there
Amid the other strangers in the sun —
A woman and an unknown man.
Wilt thou not answer me . . . but only stare
Moonward with wild eyes?

The wind lounging along the sand
   cast between them a fine dust
Smarting his eyes to tears . . .

                    Has my small ghost
That stumbled after thee so many years
So pressed its image on thy heart, that now
I am a stranger with a beard? 'Tis true
My bones were smaller when thou sawest me last,
My head a silken thistle for thy hand
To stroke and start away as from a sting
My eyes yet had in them the sunwise glow
Eyes have that do not question they are loved
But take love happily with air and food
And such sweet common things men live by.
Dost thou remember, Mother? Let this moon,
That on so many nights came in thy place
To my bleak pillow, bear
Witness how thou didst leave me in the blank room
Whose window in the wall
Looked forth upon another wall,
And how at my cry
Thou didst turn back upon the stair
And set four kisses softly — on my brow,
On each wet eager cheek — the tender last
On my small heaving breast

93

Four kisses lightly laid . . . now deep
As four nails in a cross . . .
There was significance in that sign . . . a cross
And tenantless . . . this is unique.
He made his cross to flower, mother — mine
Has arms to honor me . . . no crown . . . a crown
May grow from out the ruined trunk in time.

Did I affront thee or bespeak thee once
Without fair reverence — although I knew
That which thou fondly thought I did not know?
Did not I — clenched unto a straining ear —
Hear their feet upon the stair, who fled away
Like lice at the first light when dawn
Crept chilly-sweet from the wet fields to lay
Her blonde head on my pillow?

Didst thou feel the prickle of mine eye, fastened upon the
    doorspit —
Didst thou see me crouching like a larger cockroach
Behind the cushions of thy bed, smelling of thy lovers —
Was it for this thou didst thrust me from thy loving thought —
To spindle like a plant, uprooted from its loamy bed to grow,
Spavined and without light — that thou mightest enjoy them
    in secret who enjoyed thee?

O heart of ebony to which I had no key
Is it for thy nakedness thou durst not look upon me —
Hadst thou no garment, shameless, that thou camest naked
as the lilies?

Faugh, thou art but a rutting beast, sprawled there on the
earth's rump!
Dance, dance with thy legs agape — call on hills to enter thee!
Ravish her, O hills!
Toss her from one to the other
Till she fall without sense on thy buttocks and the night
vomit upon her;
Give her issue such as no eye hath looked upon to nourish
at her dugs.
For seven times seven and an hundred years
Let wars come out of her and famine and pestilence and the
plague of locusts;
Let her bring forth burning cities,
Till she become a symbol in Israel,
And a curse to be laid on the old wine that is poured in the
earth
When the new year breaketh;
Pierce her, O earth erect
Let thy trumpeting mountains urinate upon her their scalding
lavas . . .

Sea, mewing to Africa through the long night,
With thy multiple head swaying from side to side,
Every particle of thee living,
Mount her in raging numbers,
Sear her with thy green fires,
Persuade her with thy scales cruel as shields,
Let her cry for succor and none hear;
Deliver her
Unto the darkhead in the finned silence of thy green caves
    miles high,
Let sightless and fanged things batten upon her
Till she beat out her eyes against their darkness and become
    blind as they;
Make her known of thy serpents, thy fabulous ones men
    glimpse and not again for a thousand years,
Let these appease her.
Nay — doth she not know of these as of all abomina-
    tions —
Is there ought the sea can teach her or the dry land?
Is she not one with thee, sea — thou two darkly conniving?

O secret and oblique, with thy sweet long body filled as with
    a rank wine,
I have that which shall force thy calm and wrench from thee
    a cry.

Dost see these faces the night excretes — dost hear among
the bushes
The rattle of their hands made dry by flame?
Back, ye firelings, bide your turn
He who would bestride this darkness now must wait till I
am served . . .
Yet they come on.
The air obscenely flowers with their faces,
One but a child, a honey head, with eyes like angry wasps
Beats me with his little fists, less weight than moonbeams.
He plucks upon my hands that gird thy hair — there, I have
crushed him like a locust.
Why is this fierce aliveness in thine hair — doth April rankle
in it yet, that it strives so with my fingers?
Speak, speak! or I shall shake words from thy throat.
Give me the double turquoise of thine eye, or I will burst
light at its source . . . thus . . . thus . . .

O lambent drops that sucked the stars . . . Is this the all of
light that dies between two thumbs —
Canst thou see nought out of these pits . . . no faintest
glimmering?
Behold, O eyeless, the bloodied pearl that shall not again
take form out of thy void . . .
Let the inalienable and creeping slime from which it writhed

97

Reclose . . . over the dark norm.

                                   Hide me appalling mother!
Thou wound of time that gangrenes now, thou mud of ages,
    open and take back thy son.

3.

Warm me, mother, I am cold, so cold. Where art
        thou — is it thy breast, I lip,
           That is so smooth and rounded like a stone?
There is no warmth in it — O earth,
O hospitable earth! Let rest thy withered leaf.
Dark so dark . . . the moon is a blind eye the horizon
    lids.
Master, it is I — Judas that cries upon thee. None answereth.
No gleam, no courteous star . . . Master, I have been unkind,
Thine unjust steward who shall attend thee now. Yea I
Shall grovel at thy feet and lick thy wounds — not Mary
Had crouched before thy wounds and licked them like a
    hound.
Wilt thou not make one sign? Is this then thy forgiveness —
Thy seventy-times seven? Didst thou not say, and we all
    there assembled,

This night one of ye shall betray me.   Have I not sustained
  thee prophet —
Am I not a block set in thy temple built with words; thy word
  made stone that shall not pass away?
I say unto thee it is thou who shouldst ask forgiveness!
Yea thou, whom hills hold shoulder-high, not riding now
  upon an ass . . .
Thou, who hast made the blind to see inward into their crawl-
  ing places
And hitherto innocent corruption to become forever aware
  and armed as with a bright lance.
What hast thou found for thy lone vigils, thy tearing off of
  masks —
High crested monsters, breathing flame, to drag from their
  dark places — Nay
Small slimy things desirous to be thought fair, anxious for
  their haven of a stone or door . . .
Was it not according to thy promise I did ask and receive not,
  knock and none opened unto me?
Explain this matter, or I shall be a word shall never quite
Dissolve upon thy tongue that hath played crucible to so
  many words.
Thinkest thou, O teller of rosy lies, this moment shall endure
Within its crystaline and perfect walls us two, and not crack
  open before time?

Nay . . . love hath betrayed us both. Forgive me! I have
   covered a dark way tonight.

I belch forth words, who have been silent, as a hill

That splits asunder, vomiting on the sweet vineyards on its
   sides. O He,

Who giveth out of thy abundance and without stint,

Know I am he who taketh, having nought to give. Let thou
   be son of man

Or seed of the fierce flame that burned on Horeb, O stay my
   friend,

That men may say, of us two here alone on this landslide of
   the world, There were eleven

Petals about the rose, the fire-rose; these fell away, leaving a
   man named Judas . . .

Thou knowest best how Judas did this thing — if I be Judas
   and not some splay dark dream

Adrift in space . . . Put not thy blood on Judas, he was
   whirled,

Even as a wind blowing on a flame, by that which is behind
   both wind and flame.

Is not the olive tree hearted with cherubim, before the temple
   doors are dreamed,

And it not a cubit above ground, and was not this willed from
   the beginning?

Master, I would hear thy voice. Make me a sign . . . but
   whisper . . . I shall hear it across hills . . .

Dark, so dark, no substance for my hands to close upon . . .
  there were
Star-thistles here . . . earth slips under my feet . . . O gray
Neutrality of air, no leaf, no greening thing! There was
In all my world but one reality and that is on a cross . . . the
  cross . . . O God,
I cannot find it in this bleak nihility. Where art thou, Mother?
  Answer, I am afraid . . .
None speaketh . . . I think I cast her in the sea. Is it her
  hair
That burns with a dim animus and makes
A pale erosion on the dark? O drownèd light
Could I but reach thee I would draw thee back . . it flickers
  and goes out.

What art thou without shape or limitation that bloweth a
  great breath not wind?
O I am drawn with each deep inhalation in to be again spued
  forth
Like a broken maggot from the tongue — intake me, draw me
  with a swift suction down . . .
Whose is that laughter in the night's valleys? I once heard
Its like within a mountain pass when a great storm broke
  loose and lightning
Quivered in mid air and leapt in blinding nudity till light
  foamed from the bright dancer, thunder

101

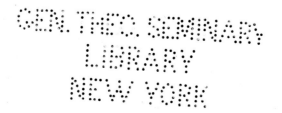

Followed along the rocks. Is't you, ye flamelings, I saw rutting in the moonlight —

One was a child with eyes like angry bees . . . was he too
one of ye?

It matters not, come hither sorry brothers, Judas will not
deny

Nor cast ye forth. But hush your laughters, I admonish
ye.

It is not meet to make merry before the crucified — did ye
not know I was the crucified?

Sing, sing, lift up your voices, hosanna to Judas in the highest

Have the young girls strew palms — bid the young girls be
light of heart

For my yoke is easy — O God of the abyss, erupt me from
this vat wherein I drip.

there is no God.

Whose is that voice, sweet and terrible — is it thine, my
soul?

Sweet soul, we have not known each other well; I have been a
busy man —

there is no soul.

What is this playful lightning in my brain, illumes a certain
garden?

Give me your ears forked friends, I have a thing to say —

Sch, 'tis a secret not for the common people — for the elect!

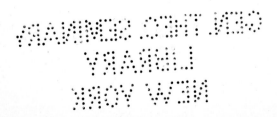

There is nothing nothing a void within a void whomsoever
Believeth on me shall be saved
                              there is no saviour
Yet remaineth a consolation
                              there is no consolation
Yet there must be a point
                              there is no point
There are these fiends
                              there are no fiends
Begin at the beginning Peter Peter beginning of the circle
  nought   there is nought   I am the rim
About the circle of nothingness   turning   turning   count
  a thousand   nought
'Twas a false start   count a thousand   nought   how does
  it begin
O God   let me remember
                        count a thousand   nought   count a
Thousand   nought   count a thousand   count a thousand

4.

Matthew
Lingered at the tree
For which his eyes
Contested with the streaming rabble of the flies . . .

He shook out of his hair
That yet tingled at the roots
As the feet of a multitude
Fidget before they rise,
The accumulated sand
The wind had dropped.
And feeling upon him the beaked
Attention of the hills
And of the intolerant sands,
Forming a ring about him,
He cried aloud to John —
Whose barley head had run along the wind
An hour gone — to hear only the swish of sand
With its monotonous and evil whisper
And the monkey chatter of the palms.
The morning was all strung with Judas' face
Impending in the nascent light — a ball
Of swarthy fire whose aborted flow,
As of a multitude there turned at bay

In its congested oval, seemed to glow
Through his closed eyelids, in whatever place
He fronted — in the sunlight, on a wall
A red and raging mote within his eye
That would not be shut out nor wiped away,
But clomb and swam between him and the sky
As it would burn forever and the day
Had oozed a bloodrop that should never fall.

Until his spirit dwindled, without will
And the cold erection of his soul
Died in him, leaving a new shame
As of a fractured innocence
He might not again make whole
But leave some part of in this place . . .

This he knew,
There facing
The selected Hill.

Till on the sweet breath of morning, the astringent
Smoke of little fires came to him, and remembering
He had not broken fast, he too went off,
Barefoot, with April over the short grass.

And light came down its shining stair
To rest on that, which like a larger mote
No longer swirled amidst the company
Of dust, assembled in the golden air,
But hung there motionless . . . yet seemed to float.
Light innocently preyed upon the face
That might retreat no further to evade
Its radiant trespass, nor evoke
The last defiance of the hands that made
This certain knot.   Light swarmed upon the rope
And kindled fire in the roan hair
That raged over the dark place
Wherein strange thoughts had spired and half things
God made out of the first slime,
Writhed upward to the light to die before his eye.

Light did not deviate its sure design
Before the stark extrusion of that head,
But came as one dispensing the last grace;
As though it had grown over time for this —
For this stemmed downward, flowering in space —
To leave on the dark flesh the ancient sign
Of its unending tolerance, and on
The lamentable forehead the old kiss —
As on the fairest king's among the dead.

IV
THE STONE

I.

Would I had been the faithful night
A seamless scabbard unto him
To sheathe his star till it grew dim
Within my dark circumference
The taper of my need;
Would I had tamed his pillared love,
Insatiate, that raped the world
And strewed it with his seed.

O I had broke the pit of flame
And poured the measure of my wrath
In on the bright aborted fruit
To make a glow upon my hearth —
To dance before, for I am whole
With no fierce hungers in my soul
For men to nail against the dawns
And worship there forever.

I have been singing . . . couldst thou hear
Through this great stone
Stuck like the thumb of Jerusalem
Against thine ear? I said,
The east is flowing at the fountainhead
Didst thou speak then, just as a wing went by?

No, I do not know what bird . . .
Canst thou make me no sign?
Lord, this is Mary . . . I am near.
Thou must not think thyself alone.
I smiled on the young guard before the gate . . . tossed him
    a favor from mine eyes to let me pass.
Canst thou forgive me that I smiled on him? He's waiting
    now . . .

She too is here who sits like curvèd tree
With cindered eyes that wear an ash
Upon them like a bloom . . . couldst thou but speak one word
To flash a bright intelligence between us two;
There is no solitude like that of two
Who sit so that they do not touch.
I cannot find her in her eyes
Save for that visible small part of her
Like the tendril that a vine
Projects through the crevice in a wall.
I think she has withdrawn to feel, as of a closed wound,
Of that within from which her lark song broke,
So long ago . . . to ring upon the world.
She is fulfilled, more perfect than a stone
The ages grind and can no more reduce
But leave, impervious, to the plodding loam.

But I am streaming all ways like a song
That dies on the progressive chord, to rise
And shake the soul again in dateless agonies.
They used me and I them . . . on those gone nights,
Such nights as prey upon me now sometimes,
Nights masking dark adventure for the heart
They place strange markings on, unbidden nights,
When flash and die strange signals on the air,
Leaving the eye uncertain of their shining,
And seem as they had crept from out some dim
First evening of the world, nights pressing close
Invading all the pastures of the flesh
On noiseless feet; rank nights whose ardors work
In men and tigers secretly, while rain
Falls through oleanders without sound,
And earth exhales an incense from her loams
And asses whinny in their stalls and slaves
Steal from out the sleeping huts to creep
Into each other's arms . . . and even old men,
Hearing the ancient tomtoms of the blood
Sounding along the darkness cannot sleep.
I have forgot most of those boys who came
And hid the faces of their dreams in me,
Amidst those mangroved waters that they stirred
And heard a thundrous singing underneath

The sluggish tides that sucked them in their flow
To spue them forth again like weightless foam.

There are dark sediments in me
And blindly swaying heads that if they rose,
Would breathe but once to die upon the light.
Time is a frenzied music in my ears
On one continuous high note . . . too high for certitudes
As though the swarming years, I ran with one by one,
Had hemmed me round
To share me in their silver company.

As they set within the temple gate
The small bright topaz of my head
That swayed and lifted when they came,
Old men with eyes that could not wait
And gallant laughter that availed
To light their sunken eyes' eclipse
And screen the trenches of their lips;
From battle grounds of memory
They brought bright gauds to pleasure me
Who warmed them at my reedy flame.

And pallid boys with hot sweet breaths
Stumbled toward me tremulously

And shook the red anemones
That brushed me with their gaudy deaths . . .
Till all the blue emollient sky
And gleaming pillars swirled with me
In dark solution in the day . . .

And they went forth with arrogant tread.
I watched their cleanly shadows sway
Like wings on the bright ground,
In breakless flight . . . and few looked back . . .
But these half turned and swung their heads
Meward like a swerving hawk,
And pierced the shadow where I lay
With light that trembled into sound;
And pulled upon some ravelling thread
In my white body like a stalk,
And did not know . . . that they were bound . . .

Even when I was a child in Magdala,
An only one; until my father died
Imprisoned in his love as in a cell,
I was a fire secretly burning.
I grew in loneliness; he drew me close
From the chance pollution of a touch; he knew
My mother's blood ran like red wine in me.

I never saw my mother.   Father said
She died, and I was weaned too soon because
I would not take the strange breast offered me.
I did not ever feel that she had died,
Who left her living presence all about,
A pressure on his heart and mine, a slow
Contagious fever in the air; and yet
It may be she did die from tedium
Of that unleavening love that overlay
Her spirit, on some night, so heavily
She did not stir when the bright morning pricked
Gently her eyelids that it could not sting
Open with the nettle of the light — did she,
Not I, sit in the temple that I dreamed
To stir and waken in a small room and find
A stranger at my side.

I used to watch through peepholes the young boys,
Whose limbs swung by like a song.   And hearing
Their voices ring, each like an ivory
Mallet falling upon my hidden keys,
Sweetly jangling, feel dimly stir in me
The lightning, the fierce knowledge hooding all
Dark secrets of the flesh.   Then on a night —
As the warm swart skin of evening burned

Between the low sun and the ascending moon
To a yet duskier rose, and I lying,
Disrobed upon the earth, no covering
Between me and the rough pelt, felt in the rock-ribbed
Gaunt body, veined of iron — it too
Perhaps cored with fire, throbbing a great pulse
And beheld dark-bearded cedars streaming
Wild upon the sky and dwarf trees, sprung
To overgrowths on which anonymous leaves
Had leapt into a stark identity,
Beetling above me . . . and the down-rushing arc
Of heaven making no noise as it broke —
There sounded a tumultuous music.
Yet I was weary when I met thee; too many
And disparate fingers plucked upon my strings
Vibrating to any touch, until the clear
Theme was lost.
                    I had not told thee all;
The words pour forth, but with a thickened flow
Like blood, not water, from some source
Invaded, that I cannot staunch.
O I have sat beside some stone
In another dawn than this . . .
And wind, slinking along the sand,
Hath crept up close and nosed my face

And licked me with a rasping tongue . . .
As this wind now . . .
                                    I faint beneath the kiss
Of fire that my lips have taken
How many times, how many times returned,
And yet burn on . . .
My throat is craterous, I am parched . . .
The wind from off the desert that hath searched
Here rooting at this rock those many hours for thee
Hath thrown its sand on me all night.

We talked a little. I felt kinder till she said,
Earth mourned for thee . . . oh why
Doth an unreasoning violence
Stir within me at her speech.
I used to wish that she would like me . . . now
I say that which I do not mean . . . I pelted
Vain words at her like pebbles . . . like pebbles
They sank into her silence and did make
Thereon no silvery ripple. The wind stirred
The hair upon her temples like gray grass
A drought hath killed, not fire. We did not
Speak again.

O see, she rocks . . . she rocks
And curves her arms out like a cradle.

The east is all but lighted, lord,
The vessel full, the lamb adorned,
Little blowing clouds are curled
Upon the forehead, yet unhorned —
O sealèd from the morning's eyes,
Light stirs within the void, a form
Yet cauled in darkness, hidden even
From hills whose tops are seen in heaven
And folded upon itself; it lies,
As blemishless as though it were
The very first born of all days
To nuzzle with its milky lips
The larger innocence of air.

O I had scaled the silver peaks
That suckle morning at their tips
And all but passed them in their flight
And I had stopped the kiss of light
Before it reached their pinnacles
That I might blaze before thy sight
With sunlight crowded in my hair
In hues too bright for eye to bear,

Save thine, inured to glory, be
A fired cloth for thee to wind
Thy loins around; that I might share,
Where eagles mate, before no eye,
And no intolerant shadow swings
Over the locked shadow of their wings,
The bread thou hast withheld from me.

Thou didst but look on me as part
Of the bright substance of a day
In memory, or as the blue
Abiding shadow of a palm
That might not lure thy feet . . . but I,
To be a thread in thy design
And spend me for thy careless use
Had shared thy vigil on that sign
That leaned so gaunt against the sky.
If on that crippled tree outspread
That bore the blossom of thy head
I might have lain, endured the horn
Of light . . . and flung me to the crucible
Of which the world is castling,
                                              the dark flame
Had used me for its further shining.

O love now I would be no mate, but mother only
And for this I hate her, who sits there,
And bore thee in her darkness like a rose
For this I would fight on and let them tear
My flesh as they have torn thy feet.

Art thou not comforted that I am here,
Dost thou seek John forever in my place?
Where is he now, thy best beloved John,
That he walks comely with undabbled hair?
He did parade before the stake, 'tis true,
At a safe distance . . . circumspectly . . . he
Sustained thy mother on his arm . . . but I
Did have no arm . . . a man must be discreet
Who bears an agèd woman on his arm . . .
Upon that night when he did speed away
He seemed a flying head in the blue air —
All serried with affrighted gold as though
The wind had broken into flower.
                                      Lord
Be not afraid that I shall follow John;
He walks alone; old, old, though he is but a boy
His blood is chillier than a fish's and his heart
Is fed with water like the moon's.   There is a fey

Thin singing in his blood
Shall trouble men, as the old moon, the unwrinkling one
Forever and silverly singing on her high rock,
Troubles the dark waters.
The song moves blind in him that yet shall make
Some pause and listen ere they go their ways
Bearing a strain of silver in their hearts
As one an alien mote within his eye,
That cannot be put forth nor yet forgot.
I hate him too . . . ah no, why should I hate
Him — who did flee off crying in the dark
He did but huddle with thy other sheep
Who would not plunge over the edge with thee
But scurried to some safer fold — Luke, James,
Philip, Thomas, Simon Peter — Peter
Moving in circles . . . but his way is power.
Not one of them had heart to learn
The wheedling ways of conquest as hath he.
How often I did warn thee about Judas —
Judas, an unsure man craving woman,
Finding in me all attributes of woman.
Had I but humoured him all had been well —
For a day, a week or summer; more
Had been a most kind fortune; Judas
Had not then needed to make affirmation

Of his little sting by thrusting it in thee
With its foul drop purpling on the dawn
Now in five spreading wounds . . . but I did fear
To anger thee, thou who hast ever
Sought to impose on me a sense of sin.
O did not all thy wisdom teach thee woman
Cannot be made to feel that she hath sinned —
Only to mime with sorrow for a mask
Wherein the bold heart holds revelry?
(How many times, O flagellants, shall we
Parade thus in remembrance!)
                         And yet
I did not once deceive thee; I was thine,
Thy conscience thou didst put cold torsion on
To walk in narrow ways.
How docilely I fell into thy hand
That plucked me from the world whose doll I was.

There was that in thine eyes, too beautiful
For a man's eyes, yet holding no veiled aspect
Of a woman's, coerced me with its male fire
All men looked at me from thine eyes within
Whose golden loopholes I have glimpsed a flame
Consuming all things unto its own ultimate
Chastity.

Have not I too made offering
Before thy dream whose altar is in air?

And arrayed in a glamourous fair dress
My soul — for thy continent delight,
For the glance, the scant word of thy praise.
I have wrought, in my body's duress,
That I be not found wanting in thy sight,
A rich garment, that I might inherit
A mansion in glory thou shouldst visit;
All the colors I have drawn from my days
In its fabric entire, that my spirit
Might be acceptable in all thy ways.

The earrings, the bracelet, the sandals of gold,
The jewels that pleasured my ears, I have sold
For thy poor — all those things thou hast scorned;
I have put no henna upon my nails,
Nor withheld one bright jot; I have forsworn
All that nurtured my beauty, fine linen
And the perfumes and the rose-colored veils
Beloved of my body that hath worn
Mean garments upon it like a pennon.
And one thing only I have adorned —

That which no man desired of me but thou,
And thou hast gone and left me desolate
In this dim garden beside her, who most
Despises me . . .
There was no joy in thee, beloved; I
Was all the laughter that did break in thee
                    And died upon the pealing.
O who now, finding promise yet in mine eyes
And no resilient darkness into which to dive
And whirl into a tranced oblivion
But the lava-dusted bottom of a cup
Whose crust hath broken into a lidless fire
But shall not turn and go forth in the night?
Better had I cindered in thy light
Which encompassed me, burning a clear ring
In which I stand cut off, a moat in time
That no light loves of passage may traverse.
                    What was that instant beam
Or bright anonymous substance that outleapt
From out the deep sockets of thy bone,
Shapely, grassed with a fine hair,
And burned up the delicate fringes of thy sight
So that I, fearing, fell down on my face
And hid me from its lashless glory?

How did I live and look upon that flame
That lightened through the air in two bright rays
That crossed each other like two swords
And fused of their own heat into one point,
And pierced some eyeball in me, unaware,
Until anguish tore at the shut lid
And bared it flinching to the light
Whereat it must forever stare,
Enduring the bright image for eternity,
Having one function and one only, to behold
The flame . . . not that which it doth shine upon.

I sense a strange infusion in this air
A fierce anarchical innocence,
(Arraign, O belly of the pit, O mouth of slime
The maggot of the light)
The flame is casketless . . . that ranges time;
The nimbus flares
I circle like a blinded hawk . . . to burn . . . to burn . .
Thy word shall burn
The generations up like corn
And hasp the ages with thy will.

O love
I see unclearly in this frustrate light
That stumbles on the rock it cannot pass,

I, here beside thee now, undone,
And all my beauty slipping like the robes
Their rude hands tore from me in haste . . .
My words are ravagings, thy word
That hovers like a burning dove
With peace upon the waters . . . hath but turned
A serpent on those lips that thou hast tamed
Not changed in their essential hungers, but made fast
And that fasting rage to foam . . . I speak in bubbles.

There came a quiet on the dawn, the wind
Falling with a lessening cadence on the sand
No longer blew her hair into her eyes
Or shook the dew-drops from the spears
    of grass about the stone.

She stared up at the glowing pallor of the sky
With steadfast look — what might not happen there
Amid those silvery far flights of air
That no hot breath intakes, where no thing dies
Or feels the little feet of fevers run
Along the narrow pathways of the bone.

She felt there flash between them a clear sign
That sped, before the eye or distraught ear

Could, pondering the gleam, identify
That which an instant shone — if it did shine —
As word or flame, or any confused sense
Aver it trembled into confluence
Of light and sound where neither ear nor eye
Might cavil at the shining evidence;
Yet leaving in her that which should burn on
Till she, out of the slowed veins' apathy,
Should look on April greening without pain
And the wild lyre of her body be
Mute upon its desolate bed — a thing
No hand should waken to voluptuous note
Or finger upon the midnights, longingly.

Whereon dripped thy wounds
Shall be roses
Cherubim shall wear in their bosoms
When they fly through the cedars
The wind shall carry the odor,

Where thou didst rest in the desert
The rocks flower,
There are wild gardens;
At the touch

Of thy hands bled whiter than almonds
The apple tree blossoms,
And the fruit thereof
Shall not perish upon the ground
For in the zone of thy breath
Bloweth temperate airs.

Thy name shall be a melody
In the throats of morning
It shall be sweet even
Upon the tongues of peacocks,
Hills shall trumpet it and the seas
Answer with a loud voice.

2.

The morning came like primroses
And pressed in through the slats
To the dim corner where He made
A rosy pallor in the straw.

I loosed the linen from my breasts
That took the light like ivory,
And pushed the door a little way
Open, and looked at him again.

The air was sweet as hay, new mown;
There was not any wind; the day
That crowded in the narrow place
Grew still to see him there.

The old men darkened on our door
One night . . . their eyes were icy-clear,
The light was frozen in their eyes
That were too bright for old men's eyes

And sided as the jewelled stars
They let in with them when they came.
It seemed as though each star did haste
To leech upon my chilling breast —

Where one had crushed a lily once
And bruised its head to give his place
And left a heavy blowth that soon
Did thrust my tender walls apart
To give its petals room.

The old men drew their shadows close
About his bed; their richen dress
Hung loose upon each thawny frame,
As spare as ribbèd lantern.

They were too tall for the small space;
Each had to bow his head.

They carried frankincense and myrrh;
They touched their foreheads to our floor
And laid their gifts beside the babe.
Their gold was bright among his hair,

As it had fallen from a star,
A petal of the light, congealed,
That glimmered on his face.

The old men said,
A fair strange star
Doth watch above the babe.
I looked up at the sky
That was of a deep purple, simmering
Like unto a brew of grapes,
And beheld a great star
By a smaller star attended.
The large star
Wore an august look; the two
Stood, mid the lesser stars

That twinkled on their shining errands
In and out the blue,
Rigid and gleaming.

I turned to the babe —
He there naked, without defence —
Saw his eyes too
Gazing without a quiver,
And put between him and the piercing
Chastity of the light
My larger breast;

I gathered unto my breast
The vast beam and the fiery
Point of the drawn star,
I felt the rays, unbent,
Streaming over the blue miles,
Grapple in my heart . . . my heart
Hath endured till now.

She sits there with her streaming
Eyes that seem to function but in tears
Mine eyes . . . are drained now as my heart . . .
There is a foolish rhythm in my blood
That circles drunkenly, my head

Doth ache worse than her head.
I am too old
To take those harrowings . . .

                    I gave
To his small frantic lips, the one
Deep need of his that I could ever fill
And wrapped him in a finer linen than I wore
                    But that was all:
There was no swaddling thought of mine that fitted him,
Who gazed at me with spaces in his eyes
Within whose shadowed deeps I seemed to see
The desert stretching out with all her stars . . .
They did not warm me with their blaze; there shone
No genial fire there to sit before
The while one wound bright threads about one's thumbs.
I have not seen such eyes in any other
As shone behind the flame-hedge of his lashes;

He was a loving child, imperious
Commanding all about him; ever
An order chafed him like a whip. I saw
Too well there would be trouble as He grew.
Nought could hush him in his angers but the sight of stars.

He would be raving in my arms and suddenly
Beholding one inshining through a chink,
Lie still and look up with that smile that always
Made me think of a still place
On some high lonesome hill, a lovely
Place to rest where none had ever rested
Or drank the air in like a snow-cooled wine.
He'd startle me with things he'd think of; once
He bade me mark one of those balls of fire
That glammer rarely upon summer nights
Marking the sunset with a deeper gold
As though the veins of evening had been drained
For increase of their luster, saying
Behold, He stoops to look upon His world
That hath grown strange so long out of His hands.
He was but five. And I remember
One eve the corn was earing and the sun
Had moved from off the pastures, leaving
Long iris-colored shadows — how He came
And bound two crimson poppies in my hair,
Black then as a lynx, and made me dance
Until I sank down on the grass. The bees
Were homing, and the legions of winged things,
That feed on the vast fig of evening, hummed,
As we sat silently, I watching

Light ambering in his big lustrous eyes.
Slowly the orchard of the sunset burned
From lime to apricot; apples of fire
Ripened and fell behind the world; perhaps He
Veiled amid His burning bushes, watched my son
Observing a clean lad of candent eye
Flawless, looking forward without fear
Even as the white ram with gilded horns
That ascendeth docilely the chosen hill . . .
We went home hand in hand . . the air
Was piercing-sweet, astringent in my throat
That almost choked upon it; the young moon
Lay on the meadows like a silver calf . . .
He was but eleven then and this
Was almost the last time He looked on me
As one half-pleased to know that I was there.

Some said 'twas John the Baptist drew him hence;
But He sought John as one entering the desert
Haileth another foremost on the trail.
Long years before the two had met I knew
That I had lost my son.

                    He had a tongue
Sided and whetted always.   There were some
Among the headmen in our little town

Who had received him, liking well his speech
But He chose ever to be with plain people
In fishermen's huts or among men ploughing
Or carriers of sheaves, and talk with them.
He liked not overly to work with Joseph
Yet He did hew and fetch and carry for him
And bear green planks yet running with the sap
That flows awhile in the cut tree.   Joseph
Could sit and plane, but when he shouldered planks
His blades, like jutting bones of an old ass,
Through his rasped skin made painful enquiry.
Oft I would say unto his sons and mine —
Good boys, submissive, did attend me well —
That which He telleth ye to do, see it is done;
Dispute not any matter with him.   Yet He grew
A stranger in our midst: his heart was dark
Or else it dazzled us with too much light;
But either way we could not look within.
I knew we were as threads, dim colors over-shone
In the large warp of his heart, that loving
All did love none wholly; than this no more:
Only a multitude could fan his eyes
To that deep blaze of tenderness
At which I used to warm me in a crowd;

To whom He spoke about deep things that none
There understood; and go home in a glow.
I have known none other have his way with crowds
As He, who moved among them like a song
Of which they were the chorus; his high head
Over-topping most other heads, his eyes
Pouring a brimming fire in their eyes
Till all their chilly emptiness was filled
And they made whole and as one family
   by his compelling
Will that drew their sundered spirits close.
My heart hath pondered this — a multitude
Diverse in all its ways, with greed lust hate,
All that dismembereth, making diverge
The mass, suspended . . . and all barricades
Of the fearful and jealous heart flung down,
Moving in majestic concord like the sea,
Habited in all its waves.   Once I observed
A silver stream of fishes on the march
In a deep river, clogging up its tides,
As they were dragged on by an invisible net,
So He drew gatherings of peoples . . . I
Do sometimes think He too was pulled dim ways
By that within him that He knew not of.

I think there was some virtue in his touch,
Though I had ills He could not free me of
As He did others.   Did I not see
In that vast throng at Capernaum
When I and my two sons pled with him to come home,
Old men throw down their crutches at his feet
And dance each with his neighbor?

                                      Yesterday
The mob approved him with a deadlier
Purpose . . . this did bewilder me who knew
His power upon throngs.   And yet there shone
Undimmed within each eye the naked blade,
Made all beholding feel as if there stood
Back of him a thousand men . . . He was the same
Who said unto one, Come, and he did follow him
And to another, Go, and he too arose
Upon the glance to flesh his word.

                                      Alas
I am too old to think upon these things . . .
Yet within me a light moveth darkly . . .
Ah me, I did not love him as a mother
Should have loved such a son.   I know this now . . .
With the chill morning coming over Egypt,
And she there with her sing-song moan
Who crieth on the light.

I think it was that in him —
Apportioned of the quick lightning that did cleave
My sapling body on an April night
And left within it graft of alien fire —
That was no part of me, I could not love enough.

I lay well out of sight of the house, the loam
Was fragrant to my hand . . . my hand
Smelled yet of the baked lamb and of the cakes made with
    honey.
It was a Sabbath eve
In April with a full moon, a wind
Frail as a kitten's paw
Played with the young grass sprung of the last rain . .
    silken
As the down upon a boy's cheek . . . I plucked
A lily and put it in my breast . . . I am an old
    woman but I remember.
Moonlight . . . white as a bride's dower . . . he came
Without sound and with gliding
    motion as a hawk wheels
But in a straight line, his eyes
Not mild nor fierce but with a queer lost light
    and tossing

Hair, the moon made silver horns among.
O folded bud of moonlight . . . and I lay
Still as corn growing . . . 'tis so long ago . . .
O sweet as many roses on one stem,
Rose heart of many thousand mornings, thou
Art she I have been seeking over the lone miles . . .
Did he speak thus . . . can I be sure . . . are hills
Sure of their jacinths, or the male light
That spends amid the hollows of the rocks
If its bright seed hath taken . . . but I know
He babbled words that fell on me like dew,
And as dew disappeared . . . and my heart
Carries them deep as the earth
Carries her jewels.

                    Odor of warm sweet breads
And of leeks chopped on the board . . .
Dim smells of musk at evening . . . O let be . . .
I am of Chaldea . . . my twilight
People to be a dusk in memory . . . I come
As out of a burst crystal . . .
Rock-fire of the slit heart . . . I am
A good Jewish girl . . . inflow
Of jewelled waters . . . shadow
Blotting the moon's disk . . . light shattering
The darkness like God's finger . . . there was pain

Fathoms upon fathoms under . . . I a vine
Threshing on the sea floor . . . up up
Out of the deeps . . . out of the moaning
Waters . . . should a mountain
Wait and the lava burning in its throat . . .
There is a white hawk . . . O tell me
Of the white hawks flying . . . there are fishes
Look up with the white eyes of blind gods . . . O tell me
Of unicorns all dripping gold down from their tongues . . .
   O stay
Whilst I pound corn and chop lamb fine in the wide bowls . . .
   a dream
Corrupts if kept too long . . . all things corrupt . . . two
   dreams
Have met here and embraced . . . he shook
The moonlight from his shoulders, the leaf-thin
Moonlight fell down on me as he rose,
A silver beam had played among his hair
Made a faint heat within my palm as though
'Twere warm yet from his hair . . . I strove
To carry it like water to my lips
And spilled it on the ground . . .
I smelled kine-droppings . . . and the sharp scent
Of the olive trees on the dusk air.
Afar off an ass brayed . . . and the bray

Was a sword, cutting my life in two.
I did not draw my linens close . . . that April
Was not cold as this . . . but lay and let the moon
Abase me with her silver hooves . . .

                                    Joseph
Was a good man, patient and as sound at core
As a white artichoke.   There was no man
Did dare make mock of me nor woman pass me
Without speaking before Joseph . . . Joseph
Brought me in his thrawn hands lilies four.
He put one lily in each hand and set
The fairest on my head above my brow
And one between the lilies of my breasts . . .
I think of him with lilies now, that knotted
Gnarled man like unto a twisted willow,
It was Joseph
To whom the light was first vouchsafed:
He had fasted many days — but eating
A sparse handful of dried figs and drinking
Water I brought to him in a stone jar,
Setting it down softly, his back turned — with arduous
Prostration of the stiff body he did hold
From any intimate touch of me — before high heaven

Made torches of the eyes of Joseph . . .

                                        Even

On that sweet night of April I had known
I had been honoured among women . . . I had dreamed
Archangel . . . above that
My dream cowered and hid its face . . . but Joseph's
Eyes, gray as afternoons when veins of day
Are swollen with the rain that does not fall
Looked without flinching on the clear light, Joseph
Had crowned me queen of heaven, an I cared
For such high place.

                        By the unfailing

Shelter of his eyes, I spun much thread
About my distaff or ground maize or corn
Or baked the little cakes for holidays.
And when He came, I was no more a girl
But a still-tongued woman, wishful
In secret to forget . . . all that was tinder
Within my heart burned up in one gone night.

He had no gratitude for service given,
Who gave unaskèd service unto man
And bird and beast and fly; when He was seven
I saw him hang over a sheer edge to save

A drowning dragonfly from out a pool.
He had no greed for gifts, He who gave all;
Our house was at the cross-roads, strangers passing
And seeing there a young strong boy would bid him hold
Their asses' heads, and He would patiently
Bide there with some gaunt beast an hour or more,
But if one laid a coin upon his palm
He would return it with a royal look.
He had a steadfast eye, I never feared
When He was there, tempest nor lightning nor the way
The writhen sands swirl, streaming along heaven
As though God haled the desert by its hair.
I thought of this last noon upon the mount
What if that hill had opened . . . and I almost
Did wish that it would open, vomiting
Its screaming multitude . . . I too
Flung upward like a stone that being hard
And remaining integrated, surely
Should hurt that which it struck . . . and it must strike
Some thing . . . I had not been amazed if earth
Had made the sign they looked for out of heaven;
I had no faith that heaven would make a sign
For him who had not kept its ancient ways.
But when I set my feet down hard on earth
I felt in her — the unchanging, the many voicèd

Who hath no foolish words, upon her tongues
Of iron, and no vain utterance
But who breaketh her silence after many years
By stammering fire out of her mountains —
Such infinite and dark vibrations
I yet feel in my heart.   And thinking of this thing
   I turned
To Mary, sitting sullen and aloof
Her wild hairs streaming like a parrakeet's
Head-feathers, silver-beaded with the dew.
Thy head is dampened of the morning, let me dry
The dew from off thine hair, I said, but she,
The dew is sweet and cool upon my forehead.
Then I — to comfort her who can have little
Comfort of her memories — the earth
Doth weep for him.   But Mary said, with that blue
   swooping eye
And glance that lancinates, The traitorous
Earth that scorpions nest in, hath no sorrow for him, He
Was pithed with other fire
Than leapeth at her core, if it doth leap
And her heart be not rock.   Did I not see
When that strange dark had passed from off the world
How dome by dome reached like a new-washed hand
To touch the sky voluptuously, and as one

Newly arisen from delirium
Earth lift herself up by each hill
And hear how her beaks of stone
Suddenly sang —
And Mary darkening looked on me as though
I were some kin of the dark earth
And hated earth because of me.
She hath a rabid tongue, that girl,
One ranteth without meaning or with ill intent
I will not speak with her again . . . and yet
I do not like to hear her sob that way . . .

There is a pallor in the east. I drowse . . .
I am too faint to watch this light in, and my heart
Hath dragged too many loads up hill to sit here now
And bear the freight of years along one night.
I would that I could sleep . . .

                    how He
Did hate to sleep . . .
Oft when I had bemused him with my song
Until his two lids, like two white moths,
Fragilely folded . . . He would start awake
And reach his arms out to the night,
Or such slight part of her as He could see

144

From out our little window . . . night
In a vast formless silence pressing
The four walls of our room . . . and nought
Between us but a taper . . . aye, He ever
Loved that which most I feared . . . crowds, night, fire,
   night
Hath tides of fire . . .

                              my heart hath lain
Too long across the currents of their flow . . .
Would I could sing myself to sleep with him
                     and rock on in a dream . . .

Light-feathers   blown from the breast of the morning
windful   by windful   tumble like snow
first-feathers   lightly shed from the dawn-wing
cling to his eyelids   do not let go.

Touch softly his lids as He toucheth the blind
yet make not too shining thy ways   lest his feet
that ever sped on with the morning behind
should strain at their bindings   too wayward his feet

for low rhythms of earth   the dim pulse of the rye
or slow tread of barley in loam or of wheat
or clog-dance of bee climbing thigh on gold thigh
from the flower of saffron   still let them lie

swaddle him downily   hide him from sight
wash his pale hands in the milk of the light
hush his wild tongue   on the strings of the sky
sounding its stammering fifth   let him lie

under the light-droppings   almond tree deep . . .

V
PETER

I.

Peter shivered in the early day
   Whose shining presence did not make him warm,
   And he, there pondering its lucent ray,
Arranged upon his knee, an ordered form
Of light aquiver that his shaking palm
Might hold suspended but not deviate,
Was stirred to wonder how he did create,
With the bubble of his breath, a vacuum
That time should circle, not assimilate;

A bubble on which all light should play
And the renascent colors of each day
Circulate in many a giddy dance,
Making it glitter in men's sight; a sphere
Surrounding nothingness as with a glass
From whose bright surface should forever peer
The shrunken image of his countenance.

He drew his knees in, gathering his feet
Well under him and folding his arms tight
And strove to warm before the charmèd light
Old days had left in him his chilly heart
To start as at first touch of a hair shirt

149

To find the virtue gone out of each part
And all their wraithly sunlight without heat.

He thought on a great-eyed fish he had caught once and
    quailing
Under its silvery stare, flung back into the sea;
Of a man the sea snared, in his own net
Entangled like a fly, and leisurely
Ate as he looked on, who thought, now I shall dive for
    him . . .
A moment . . . and I go . . . and had not gone . . .

And how as he walked home the waves had raced
Beside him iridescently, outpaced
Each other to his feet, and peacock-wise
Outspread in plangent greens before his eyes;
How veering gulls, that wheeled above the Place
The waters covered with their seamless silk,
Had gleamed as though afire in the blue haze
That hung like smoke over a sacrifice;

Till that day too had burned in gold and blazed
Along its darkening edges, ray by ray
Dwindling upon the waters; till it closed
Softly upon the twilight like a flower
And passed . . . as even this should pass away.

2.

Peter lay face down in a valley between hills.
Feeling over him a weight as of mountains
He could not lift up his two eyes that were buried in the
sand
Nor stir from off the earth that held him like her dust.

He felt a gaunt heaving, a devouring, a dark separation in the
body of the world that was strangely too his body;
This troubled him until he remembered
I am Peter the Rock, the rock, the word swelled in him like a
seed;
Rock-word thrown up by the great mouth vomiting.
Ach! earth retched with his immense nausea.
Rock hurtled, seeming hard, tender and aching,
To burst into the shoots, into the marble columns
Stone . . . stalking up and up in perpetual adoration;
Granite for thy flowering. I am Peter the rock, the basalt of
thy garden . . .
Earth . . . quickening in the quarries, under the ribs of iron
He too humbled yet proud under the mountains:
O mighty I am of thy thews . . . he stumbled on the flame
edge, piercing
His hands, too, and forehead, hanging head-down, O lancinat-
ing

Flame burning on forever and without end!   Gaunt frame of
  earth
Labouring under the scarped places, light
Streaming into cavities — O stretched apart, ye also
Strings that He hath smote on with his singing thumbs,
Shall not ye too make offering?   He tasted
Stone-dust on his tongue and the brackish
Tangs of the raw ores — I too am rock, I am a cleft rock, the
  light
Hath chosen for its sacred uses.   Tip-tapping
Of thousands upon thousands of picks upon the mountains
Linked chain of the black white yellow brown bodies down
Into black pits, into the quarries, like the dry white mouths of
  fishes, down
Into the guts of hills — is it your blood O brothers
Sprinkled on the granite, oozing out of the white mortars?
What an ye flow — hath He not made all men brothers
And shall not your blood run together?   Why answer ye not,
  me,
O children of one father, your feet sliding on the declivities?
(Blood too on the white robe, on the body under the robe . . .
  did He not say, O virgins,
I come not to bring peace among ye but a sword?   (Mediate
Between me and his heaven, white heads of stone, O hands of
  granite, pray for me!)

Shall not the marble be ensanguined, veined of your arteries
    O brothers —
I Peter, fisher of men, hooked amidst your gullets?
I am a common man, a man of action: truly
Had He not called . . . I should have led ye, even as Judas of
    Gamala.
Things for me already ended, at Genesareth, and the sea
    staled upon me,
I weary of the platitudes of her waters . . . hearing
Under her numbers my people crying. Had the sons of
    Zebedee
But cast in their lot with me I had been gone, but Salome
Coveting the luster and the glory, did fear me who was a
    crested hawk, her sons
In pinfeathers; and I did falter to go forth alone . . . my
    boats
My wife, warm hearth, the Sabbath feast . . . stuffed fish upon
    the table . . . when He came
All melted in that stream through which we flowed that bore
    me like a leaf past my own door.

Judas . . . dost thou too burrow, doth wide earth, hiding all
    who have in them some wormy thing to hide
Betray one unto the other? A darkness writhing . . . moving
    not of its own will . . . he bubbleth

Upon shining waters . . . on that current none may leave or
  leaving
Move again with the slow even pulse of things . . . why dost
  thou call on me, who have not liked thee ever,
Though I did smile on thee sometimes — because none else
  did and I knew
Thou wouldst best tender service for a smile. But one did
  love thee,
He who loved all men . . . didst thou not know this fool?
  All still . . . three times he rose . . .
I think he hath gone down for the last time.

Brothers

There were twelve men and one of us the man Judas . . . look
  to this thing
An ye gather in secret conclave; ponder each other's faces;
Especially and there be one none love but all men suffer
  merely . . .
I had aroused ye, brothers, believe me, I had poured
Fire in your ears until ye had arisen — ye behind me. I had
  freed Judea, yea, Peter, who henceforth
Shall speak but with His accent . . . I am a plain man, un-
  learned
But I say unto you this day prophecy is upon me! I am Peter
  the Rock, I socket
Pillars, I sustain temples! Uphold me brothers, I am Peter,

Slitter of the throats of fishes — hoist me upon the stone

Antlers, horning azure, taking the light upon their tips. O I
am the word

Made rock to watch above the peoples, that shall pass and look
up at me as they pass —

Incessantly drifting as sands of the desert under my stone
lids . . .

Before me, Peter and no other . . . I say there shall not be
another! yet one moveth

A force pallid, without color, as a wind blowing over earth,

Yet fiercely and with direction . . . not of thy dark flesh, O
mother, not in him shall thy perennial

Aprils fasten and make house; he is not of thy enduring

Bone . . . not on him shall it be founded but perpetuate
through me, Peter, the Rock . . . seeded with his temples.
Fire

Descendeth from above until the tree is cleft and the honey
thereof spilled upon the ground . . .

Shall not the wasps gather? We are a cloven generation . . .
in us devastation,

In us the fire and the begetting of fire — What of it bantlings?

Shall ye not arise, shall not your day too lighten,

Before ye and in ye and after ye the fire?

— I am seeking, seeking . . . that stirs, in me that I cannot
touch,

He did have knowledge of . . .

This in commemoration, O Master, I shall nurture

That which thou didst cast upon the waters and in stony places,

As in the pebble, in the drop poised upon the thorn . . .

Behold, I bring forth as a garden . . . lilies unwithering,
  magnolias of iron.

Together brothers, to the beat of your little hammers, to your
  anvils singing

Keep time with your hammers, O anonymous — earth hath
  that in her she must be rid of!

Ye too Essenians — shall we not adore the sun together?

I tell ye He is one with the light that gladdeneth.

Will ye not sing, O Fasters, who aborteth the song within
  ye — did not our people

Sing of old unto the harp and with cymbals; they remembering

Songs in their captivity, and are not threnes in the Jew's heart?

I tell you this day there is vision in me, I tell you

There shall be those who come after you shall have song upon
  their lips

Hundreds of thousands upon thousands swarming

In the cavities of those hills that are so steep and straight

They all but meet above me . . . brothers, have I provoked
  you,

Backs turned quietly working, that ye will not look upon me

On whom ye shall build his church that shall also be my
    church — is it that the harlot
Entereth the holy house?   But I say unto you, the harlot
Is the last word made woman, not even He shall put away . . .
There were many such did follow him up the steep hill . . . ah

Can not I silence amid stone that hath closed upon so many
    cries
Dawn-cry of thy cock?   O master, I have seen winds upturn
Fishing boats, and rend with their strong webbed feet the nets,
Returning unto the sea her silver company — is there no wind
Can break the bubble of this breath that hath denied thee?
O I am a coiling and dark place, not still
And yeasty cries come up out of my depths.   Assoil me, let not
    thy enemies destroy
That brand hath been ignited at thy flame.
Uplift, I beseech thee, the carrier of thy light.   Though I did
    flee
In darkness I have held thy flame that is in me and shall be
    blown on and yet not put out.
Didst thou not say the son of Man did have no place to lay his
    head
And hath not the word lived in me as a reproach?   Now I shall
    build thee many habitations
Beautiful as the towers of Tiberias, and more impregnable,

Whiter than snows of the North peaks I shall uprear thee
Ramparts of the snow that doth not melt . . . on thy stony
   body, earth;
It stretched along the Great Sea like a vast eye watching,
Cupolas upon seven hills . . .

            White hands of marble, pray for me . . .

3.

Peter beheld the paradigm
   Of light that on his palm did sit
   Arise, a glowing bird, and wheel
Three times about his head and then
Make itself small and enter him

By unused way and secret lane
It made its way up to his head
And whirled amid the pillared frame
Of ivory, that could not spread
To give its pinions place;

Around and round the tiny flame
That burned therein, on whirring wing

158

That ever turned and never moved
From out the circle tightening,
There spun the golden bird of pain

Around about the shining thing,
The riddle of the light it loved . . .
And he had all but solved . . . and grooved
A path of fire within his brain.

The wind blew in salt from off the Dead Sea: Peter
Lifted his gaunt body shaking the ray from off his hand down
    on the floor . . .
He said, I have been ridden as I slept; I would I were recon-
    ciled unto my people,
Shall I go back to Bethsaida and down unto the sea again —
    nay all
The waters of Genesareth cannot quench this fire hath been lit
    in me . . . I must go on.

VI
THE MERCHANT OF BABYLON

I.

Myrenne?
                    Yes Sargon
                         We love each other?
We love each other, Sargon.
                                   Put thy face
Near me, little jasmine. Art thou not glad
I am a mouth yet warm against thy mouth,
Two hands still whole upon thy hands?

Should thy mouth be not warm and thy hands whole
That hath not done a wrong to any man?
Did it save him, that his had wrought no hurt?
Hush, hush, thou must not brood upon this thing
Lay thy head here and I will stroke thy hair
Till thou shalt sleep; 'tis almost dawn.
There is a man spread on the sky —
                                   Were there not three?

I see one only;   whose enormous
Shadow darkens upon Jerusalem
Folding all other shadows in its girth.

I should have gone with thee up the ascent
Or kept thee here within my arms; I hate
This forward city of Jerusalem

And all its blindwhite stone and its bare hills
That do not wear a tree!   When may we leave
For Babylon?
                    The week after the feast.
The rare and shining fabric, shimmering
In many colors, for the temple veil
Hath been delivered and in good time
Before the golden gates; and I have yet
Grave matters to attend on — but for these
We should leave this stony city, brandishing
Her marbles and her god-house roofed with gold
That rampant in the sun of yesterday
Did so abrade mine eyes that they did loose
Their little waters on the sight.   The Romans
Do sneer at that on which they most depend;
And merchants, once esteemèd in this city,
Are overtly disdained;   this is not all:
Ill smells do congregate, and undisturbed
The litter hath its way upon most streets;
Then there is meager stabling for the camels
With these full caravans inpouring
And meaner for the slaves.   Did I tell thee
Last night we lost a slave — the sickly one,
Who ran behind the camels?
                              Did he escape again?

Yea, and for the last time: his fellow slaves,
Contending each for place to lay his head,
Made brawl upon his chest while he did sleep
And stopped his little breath.

                                    Ha ha ha ha ha!
It is no laughing matter, Myrenne,
I am man-short and men are costly here.
Even in Babylon a chesty slave,
One sound of limb, with two good eyes and all
Or nearly all, his teeth and no gangrene
Will bring twelve shekels in the market.

I am sorry thou hast lost a slave,
And sorry for the slave . . .

                                    But thou didst laugh.
O Sargon, I am sitting here alone
All day; now I am weary, let me sleep.

Sleep, sleep . . . all that thou thinkest of is sleep
And threading opals in thy walnut hair
Or putting on pomade . . .

                                    Yet He did speak
Of woman as a man might of his own friends!

Would I had known him then.

It was not by my judgement, Myrenne
That we did come upon the Passover
Thou wert so wishful to behold —
                              Let be!
Must thou upbraid me that thou canst not sleep?
Soon we shall have a child and then I cannot
Take those long journeys but sit at home and grieve.

Dost thou not want a child to bind our hands
Fast with his smaller hands?
                              I do not know . . .
I know I am a closèd pod about thee
And when thou leavest me but a split rind
Emptied of all good.
When first I did love thee thou wert small in me
Who now hast grown and filled me as a seed
Swelling in April fills its jar with bloom
Whose leaves do fall before the blossoming.

Shall galleys miss appointments with the tides
And tarry on their courses, caravans
Dawdle on desert ways that thou art fair?
                              Aye, I am fair —
Not like thy dark-skinned women
Who show off well thy gold, upon their arms

That worketh on some skins until they glow
As with a dusky fire underneath
My hair not black nor gold, mine eyes not blue
Nor tinted with a Tyrian purple —

Nay, thou hast the bloom upon thee of first fruits
Thine eyes are like the early mist on hills
Before the mist is broken.

                      I am as mist
To be cast off thy day with the first light.
How shall I stay forever by thy side?
Forgive me that I was unkind. This night a thing
Doth lean like crossbeams on me, that my heart
Must drag along its route.

                    Thou who hast gazed
So long on him, tell me how He did look.

He had a lusty frame but scant of flesh;
There was a farther shining in his eyes
As they had looked too long upon some light
Glimpsed upon the rims of vision, with such stark
Intensity the crystals of the sight
Had burned up in that instant fire
Which cooling left a constant image there

To trouble eyes that not again shall see
Overly clear for the bright shape
Between them and the floating dust.

Did none attend him, did He die alone?

I saw but one of those young gainly men
Who made such brave showing at the temple
That I had thought they would have cast their lives
As one throws flowers at admired feet.
I doubt if they did wholly know his purpose
Or see their way by that which dazzled them
As doth a too bright light by very shining
Obscure all things that lie before those eyes
Within the circle of its radiance.

Was there no woman?
                              Some two or three; I noted
A girl with hair like a burning bush; an older
Woman whose eyes were like unto his eyes
As darkened lamps to those lit with a flame.

Did not the people grieve to see him so
And did she weep, this girl who followed him?

Her back was turned to me I only saw
The drooping shoulders and red blaze of hair

The people . . . were like fasting lions . . . they
Had torn him an they had their will. In truth
He was a darker leaven in the world
Than any knew even of those old men
Who harried Pilate into action; they
But felt, and shook unto their gnarlèd roots,
The cherished symbols He had overthrown
Wrench, as do falling pillars at their piles,
Hard upon the withered vine of thought
That twined about the ruin . . . but no more.
There was a common danger for our kind,
Who hold brute forces of the race subject,
In him who did proclaim all men were brothers.
That was no thought to put in a slave's heart.
There have been fierce uprisings among slaves
Whose frantic hordes may overrun the world
Dismantling that which we have made so fair.

Did He not mean it would be thus in heaven?

An they shall brother angels in high heaven
Shall they not ask fair courtesy of men
Here on the lower earth, and if the spirit
Straighten to its full height, shall not all parts
And planes of that in which it is implicit

Aspire unto its valiant company?
I beheld, behind a pillar, listening,
In the first court of the temple a young slave
Who let his tray of fruit spill on the ground.

If this man had so much mischief in him
Why art thou sad that He is gone, Sargon?

There was incautious splendor in his look
As the vulture fell like a flung stone
Hurtling out of heaven . . . I functionless
Stood there disjoined from nature like a tree
Whose root is traversed by an alien heat

Art sure the vulture . . .

I am not sure.   There was a dark cloud; two lights
Leapt toward each other . . . to mine eyes it seemed
Two flames had mingled in the firehead
And stammered lightning . . . I did not look again
But something swooped and his eye had no fear
There was that in his look that blinded me
So that I stumbled going down the hill

Didst thou not look back?
                                    He who would peer

Into the craters of an eyeless god
Must have strong sight, unhooded will erect . . .
He gave a cry as I went down the hill
That sank a javelin in my heart . . . and yet . . .
O I am half ashamed to tell thee this;
As I walked homeward through the narrow street,
The way that runneth parallel to this
One played upon a zither — a light tune
That urchins whistle as they run . . . it seemed
The sweetest music I had ever heard
Why was this thing?
                              Thou didst feel happier
To know there was a light heart in the world.

It was not that —
                    Nay do not vex thyself
With thinking on this man.

In him man's image waxed unto god-size.
Gods should be made with hands, whittled of wood
Or carved in stone or poured of bronze or iron
Not freed from the harsh fires of the soul.
In Babylon . . . O my city of fallen
Gods . . . our gods had many counsellors
Nor troubled over much with their stone eyes

The darkened corners of the spirit. I
Do well applaud such gods who do receive
Flesh offerings, leaving the spirit whole.
 Myrenne, I drowse . . . stroke thou my forehead
 With thy cool fingers like a little wind . . .
O dust, Jehovah bloweth with His breath!
The dove alit between thy breasts, Ishtar,
In divine intimacy with thy stone
Flesh, hath died in its cold nest . . . Babylon
Thou, too, worn down as a great rock seas beat
Till it is ground small, small as a pebble . . .
But none can broider the fine cloth for mantles
As we do yet in Babylon . . . Babylon
To be as a garden for this hardy tribe,
Spreading like a rank vine upon all grounds.
Jehovah,
Thou also of the dark fires — how many
Souls have gone into Thy casting, Molten!
 Stroke, stroke thou my hot brow.
He too a Jew . . . Jew's hands upon our gold . . .
They leave their signature on that they touch
Who touch not lightly . . . crowned head of a Jew
Thorn-chapleted . . . abasing Caesar's . . . this
New coin may wear too well . . . why must a Jew
Presume a light and follow to the nail's end

172

To root in darkness . . . He who is nailed
And He who nails . . . this integral in each
The vision and the beak that rends . . . with these
The circle closes, flaming at the breach
Until the stark neutrality of night
Descends on both . . .

Why did He not cry on the poor people
He had so often healed of their vile sores?
Did not even the holy Zoroaster
                              lay waste his enemies?
It had not availèd, Myrenne,
Had He led slaves He had been first to die
When they had gained their goal and an ended
Dream had spired unto farther flowering
In him, for whom all roads led to the stake:
Great love must find equation in great love
Or else in hate of a like stature; he
Who hath no equal in desire must surely die.

O speak no more upon this matter, rest
Thy head upon me.
                    Aye I must sleep.
What boots it to let day overtake me
Bustling on her thousand ways nor wasting

A look on any fallen out of step.
Here in this city is no weakening,
Resolve, hard surety of stone . . . to be
Uptorn perhaps, hewn, carried off in blocks
But not disintegrate to final dust,
Unless by smashing it to atoms, then
By these same processes, of air heat light
In which elemental things achieve
Volition, to again meet, touch, cohere,
Dimension, force, aim, all the shapes of dreams
Implicit in the mass, the grains of dome
And pillar again to be pillar and dome . . .
     Would I could sleep . . .
Night, in those shining galleys of the stars
Doth carry her large business on
                         and I must look to mine.

Come with me to this tiny window — see
The white stones of Jerusalem that seem
More kindly in this light.
                              Jerusalem
Accouched and resting comfortably . . . whatever score
Time doth mark down privily to make
Wild music for another day . . . dark, dark
As indigo, so still . . . the secret there

Up in those glimmering far flights of space
Where infinite bright things transpire . . .

                                 O cease

Thou art not he whom I knew yesterday —
Lightheart, urbane, with largess for a slave
Pride before equals and grave courtesy
Unto strangers, bowing but not too low
To thy superiors: now a strange man
Thou liest darkly at my side.

                         Aye mine
Hath been the hill-less, unperilled way;
But once I toiled up an ascent, no more . . .
My will is castrate, pliant as a worm
And, caught between two forces, must excrete.

2.

Sargon!   (she screams)
             Yes Myrenne, my Myrenne,
       What is it, what aileth my beloved?

Sargon, It stirred!   there is a silvery
Whisper upon the morning.
                           What did stir?
The child, our child, it leapt in me —
                                O string
That lay as thou wert not until our two
Wild fingers plucked upon thee . . . Myrenne,
Come close and I shall fold thee tight, so tight
Thou shalt feel nought within thee but my heart.

Why dost thou look through me with such strange eyes
As I were loophole in a wall and thou
Beholding that which doth appal thy soul —
What seest thou in me?
                       The end . . . the end . . .
Coifed in the bright beginning . . . Myrenne
A shadow doth out-stride me . . . shall we two
Go forth to meet it in each other's arms,
Drift now beneath its feathered darkness, closing
Softly about us, shutting out the sky

And all the bugling stars and the arousing
Fanfare of the sun?
                              And what of him
I carry and who cannot save himself?
All night thou didst cry out on the old gods,
And now on Moloch to give him our son —
Or for that Man they nailed against the sky
But yesterday? I, too, see him now, I see
The bottomless holes in his two palms
We must pour our three lives in — One calleth
A name in a clear tone like a silver
Trumpet!
                    None did call, Sweet, calm thyself
Or we shall have the inn about our ears.

Yea now 'tis thou who wouldst hush me! O He
Hath heard thee Sargon, He doth turn his head
This way, seeking for thee and me, his eyes
Do delve for me like lightning in this room.
He calleth not on thee — He spake the name
Of our sweet Thaddeus —
                                        What Thaddeus?
Him I do carry in me darkly curled.

O foolish one, may 't not be Myrenne?

Nay, a male child shall be named Thaddeus.
He summoneth to follow on the way
That is made terrible with too much light
Thaddeus, the unborn! he to go singing
Up the ascent of earth, unto the steep
Place and into the dark burning . . . hide me, hide
Me from his eyes that yearn —

                              Thou ravest, love —
Bury me in a deep cool place, my heart
Is smoking in my breast, I die, I die!

Thou dove that nestleth in my hand and I
Forgot a moment and did clench my hand!
Let nought disturb thee, I am here —

                              O He
Did call on Thaddeus.

                    Dear Myrenne
He is a dead man and can do no harm,
His words are dust —

                    Didst thou not say that dust —
O I did babble in my sleep; forget
That which I spake.

                    Thou didst not hear
Him call upon our son?

                    A dry leaf, wind

Let fall upon our sill as it passed by,
Made rustle in my ear; all else was still.

O now thou art the Sargon that I know
I am no more afraid.
                          Thy tears have washed
The shadow of the Cross away; the light
Hath gone about its farther shining . . .
And I would sleep now for a long long time . . .
Dwindling, dwindling, the trajected ray
Transcribing a vast circle . . . sing to me.

O lay upon my tender breasts thy head
That bruiseth them like bronze, and I shall hush
Him, whose rosy flesh within my flesh
Doth stir no more, and thee upon one song:

3.

To sleep, to sleep, the web of dawn
    Hath broke upon the eastern gate.
    This bay-blue vase that cups the night
Within its fragile hollow, soon

Shall tremble into beauty, now
It all but shimmers, luminous,
As though light hidden in the clay
Had dimly stirred to meet the light.

To sleep, to sleep, O do not wake!
Morning is a bird set for flight.

The dawn, that seeketh lightsome thing
To rest her early pinions, yet
Unused to flight — O do not speak —
Hath drifted softly on thy face

As on the first wild bird to fly
Alone where pearling waters stretch,
And resteth on thy olive cheek
As on thing most fair for light to touch.

To sleep, to sleep, the marble wings
Are pointed toward the amethyst

O put thy head upon my breast
Where all night long the moon hath lain
As quiet as a silver dove
To brood on thee and bring thee peace.

Soon shall the temple roof upfling
A golden gleam as though one mane
Of a thousand lions lying down
Had lifted in the wind — O come

And let thy head be my heart's guest
And rest on me and do not move.

VII
THADDEUS THE UNBORN

I.

Light
    Came like a broadsword in through the slit
    Of the squat window, lay flat-up on the
bed,
Suave and shimmering and of a smooth edge
A child might play with. Slowly Jerusalem
Reared her multiple head, rauched behind facades,
Serried with little cries, turned upon her stone
Hams, sweated and stank; feet shuffled to and fro,
Voices hummed and honed, uttering no thing
Of import in any tongue. The room was a floating
Bubble of silence amid the arc of sound
Enclosing its fragile walls as the sea
Enfolds a shell, it holding like the shell
Infinite murmur. On the bed the two
Lay, like emptied vessels, on their sides
Drained of all save dreams. Only the two breaths,
Interlacing, imperceptibly wove
Patterns in the stale air and dispersed
Gently, without friction.
                 Myrenne gazed
Before her with wide eyes of the color
Of sea-water cupped in a rock; the naves
Had grown and spread upon the iris; night

There had a last foothold. Like a dark stone
The head of Sargon lay between her breasts
That gleamed like broken marbles in the light.
The light had taken on a bright edge, it bore
Downward like a naked blade, dissolving
In its gold the gray sheath of air. She saw
The cloak, of Sargon, embroidered in silver
Spread upon the chair, her rose-colored veil
Stirring a little, the gossamer
Wings of flies, all these
Infinite familiar motions masking
Suspension of some vaster movement, even
Bolder because of it; objects in the room
Had taken on strange dimensions, the blue
Vase was shimmering, a stone of fire
Throwing out flames impalpable as steam,
Till it seemed the air must ignite . . . stillness
Leeching upon the heart that shrank far back
At bay in its ultimate corner . . . silence
As at the core of a jewel . . .

                                  He moved
With a large free life in the still air, blond
Hair flowing out straight as though the wind
Had fleshed itself. There was an innocence
In the eyes of the nature of the ray

That hovered upon the wall, detained there
But not to be deflected from its path.
She marked the sapling body and the male
Virginity of the mouth, sweet and apart,
Felt a cry rasp at her throat,

                              Thaddeus!
The boy trembled and turned back; he bent
Tenderly above her. She saw the young
Gaunt throat working, the big apple, the high
Cheekbones, set-back shoulders, the surpassing
Sweetness of the glance;

                              What did He say to thee?
Go forth and work among the people, aid
My perishing.

                    Thou shalt perish with them.
Thou wilt be a brand for his consuming?

No matter. I shall blaze before I darken.

What answer did thou make unto him?

                                        I said
How can I leave her whom I love, and He
When thou meetest a woman on thy way,
Thou shalt know thou dost behold thy mother.

He divideth peoples,
He putteth near hearts asunder.
O He hath raped my son out of my womb!

The blue vase threw out a faint heat, Sargon
Stirred and murmured brokenly in sleep
And as one who is very old put forth his hands
As though to warm them at the flame,
It is the male ardor in thee, the dark force
Harmless as a sheathed blade until some call —
It may be but a bugle slavering
The morning with beguiling silver tongue —
Doth give to that which moved directionless
Identity and aim. It is the blind
Purpose in the soul whereby men go
Singing to all wars

Myrenne: And women flee
Into the loving arms that rip their babes
From out their wombs on a spear-point to trace
Brave patterns for the male dream.
Sargon: Chaos is in us as at the beginning
And darkness and light mingled, but in her
Is a dim serenity. Before man
She was, who is co-eval with the worm

And the green herds of the waters that did flap
Their vast ears at the morning. Thy smooth hair
Is soft as sea weed, Myrenne.

                              Shall I give up my son
Because some man amid a crowd doth rave
And cry upon him with leper's tongue?

Not one, but all the thousand, thousand men
Shall walk upon our dust when we are not,
Do call me mother, through that voice I heard
That plucked some heavy substance from my ears
And rent the protective covering from off
My heart, and left me a stripped nerve wherewith
The paining tendons of the world connect.
'Tis for the race I leave thee.

                              Thou art young
And so the dupe of numbers, Thaddeus,
Too young to estimate their tyranny
And know the chastity of the deep source
That draweth in all tributary
Streams, but to augment them with its flow.
First there is one who taketh to himself
Another . . . and from junction of these two a
    third
In time doth spring; this is the race, the race

That jetteth from all points upon the world
And over whose destinies the gods do hold
Their secret counsels.

                There is but one God,
He who is pithed with light and hath upspewn
Man from his entrails.

                Then thou art he,
My son, my son, for whom God made the world
So beautiful; the young grass to flower
Perennially with lilies and the good grains,
For thee dissolvèd in the veins of fruits
His high ethereal blood to make thee dream
On in a pleasant madness and forget
The clenchèd movements of his wrath, for thee
Made marble blossom in the quarries, gold
Artery the faithful rock and iron
Rib the dark mountains and enjoined
Earth bejewelled for thy glistering,
Froze moonlight into silver and ordained
The worm to weave thy tunic and all beasts
To yield thee pleasant service — why must thou
Amid a thousand valleys, vineyarded,
Presume one fairer than all these?

                      Mother

It is not to the fabulous valleys

That I fare nor toward the ambrosial
Pastures that I set my face, but to lean ways
Where is no food for eagles, an their wings
Sicken upon the scarped rock.

                              But this
Is madness.
                Aye a madness contrary
Unto thy little taut hysterias . . . dear
I pray thee do not ponder my too wild imaginings.
Rest here
Beside my father who doth stroke thy hair
And will not leave thy side for very long.

Is this how thou wouldst serve the race,
To lead them to some icy fastness of the rock
Deposit there his perishing?
They had been safer with the lions.
                        Mother, mother
My aim is not yet clear to my own heart
And less to thine.   Say 'tis not for the race,
But for the self, my self, the race in me.
O now our two words join, making half sphere,
The other half all dark yet shadowed there,
Dimly, as the circumference of the moon
Ere she hath grown out to her rims.   I know

There is some thing I need, to make me whole,
I hunger for . . . O there is that within
The light, that falls alive upon the loam,
Pulleth on the dark seed till it flower;
So when I heard his call there stirred in me
Some deep bright thing that lifted up its head.
O my words shame me! I am but a boy
And thou, versed in the wisdom of old things
I have not known, listening with that smile
I cannot fathom. When I look at thee
I feel a thousand winters in my bones
And all the rivers that have ever froze
Running beneath their ice. There is singing,
I think I heard it long ago, a voice
Old, older than the world that singeth on.

Sargon: It is the solemn sound of thy own heart
          Companioning the large dim hearts of things.
Myrenne: Mine, mine, these are the tunes I sang to thee.

She sang to me, not thee, she did upbraid
Me for thy coming, Sargon said, his face
Seemed slowly turning into stone, but Myrenne
Was a dark flowing.

              It does not matter; hers
Is not the voice I hear, Thaddeus said,

And looked upon her tenderly.
Hers, hers, none else.

Sargon: All voices meet in her and inly swell
In secret chorus and she doth divine
All hearts for all hearts beat in her. But one
Door is made fast, before her inner eye,
Where through the lightning may pass . . . and she
Not gaze upon it and go blind.

Myrenne: O frustrate,
Are ye not glutted yet who die to touch
A glowworm for your star?

Thaddeus: O peace,
O quiet of the root, O ultimate
Serenity, I come, I come!
He stood, an arrow headed for the sun
A wand that seemed as though it must ignite
Touching the current of the beam, then swung
Lithely to the door and stopped half way
As though pulled on by a tightening string.

Myrenne: Then snap the cord between us, let me die.
From the low harsh voice all the beguiling
Music had been taken as the soft green
Color had been drained from out her eyes,
Two hollow caves in which black waters sank

Lower and lower, baring the white bones
That had been covered decently. Thaddeus
Turned to look back, ran toward her with a cry
And Sargon in his sleep smiled:

                                        He is slave
Of love that centereth in entity
Other than his own, and cannot flow
Outward from the small circle of the will
That doth hold it jealously apart
This . . . the last impurity of purpose . . . one
Drop from out thy heart, let with a word
Fall like a hammer on his heart, sufficed.
Exult, my Myrenne, thy potent drop
Hath spread on the horizon . . . I behold
Through my closed lids a fire on the sky
That burneth outward . . . yet remember
He will go forth again . . . there will be a last
  time.

2.

Safe, safe upon my breast.   She stroked his hair
    That overlapped like feathers, tress on tress
    Until the shining of his head grew less
And there was no rough place for hand to preen
And cozen with a touch; it might have been
A tuft of golden plumage that she wore
As she might any bright wing on her dress
That should not rise up in disturbing flight
And fly from out the window and the door
But dwindle in the morning and make one
In length and breadth with the design, the sun
Wove leisurely from out its formal fires
In thread on shimmering thread, that dallied there
With her white breasts as it did with the spires
Or on the white buds of the magnolias
Or other impediment of loveliness
That causeth light to tarry on the course,
Predestined, it must finally traverse.

O come, my eager little one
Who leapeth up to meet the light,
To sleep, to sleep, the chariot
Of day, out-raceth thy delight.

195

Thou mayest handle the bright mane
And lay thee down between the paws
And put thy head into the jaws
Of ivory that shall not close —

But do not heed the voice that soundeth
Through the hollow of the wind.

Do not let those eyes that bend
On me their awful shining, find
Thee and consume thee with their love;
When He calleth silverly

Do not answer to thy name
Serpents writhing on the sand
To thy touch shall be made tame —
But never love, O never love!

To sleep, to sleep my little son,
Hide in me and do not move.

VIII
THE BONDMAN

I.

There was little to be seen, from the boughs of the
cypress where the boy clung, nought but the forkèd
Shape no bigger than a doll against the burning arc of
sky and, on either hand,
Set lower a second and a third, the three making a triangle; on
the hill the crowd
Might have been a dark growth the wind stirred sluggishly on
the bald crown of earth —
No bigger than a thumb print on the rim of azure that was
misted as with a vast breath.
It was a chubby hill; for hours he had watched scurry up its
haunches
Little black figures that were like beetles but less nimble and
seemed to attach one to the other
Until the slow-moving line stretched about the crosses like a
snake.
He saw the undulations of the jointed body that seemed pulling
at his own
And felt its dim and angry vibrations, saw the multiple
Head, of which he was a forlorn and unassembled eye,
Sway, torpidly iridescent, and made signs upon his skinny
fingers,
Urging to some gaudy action, that which was enraged and
quivering

And yet that did not strike. Now he turned from this coiled
    inertia of the crowd
To the gliding silence of the vulture, that was a darker
Spark of the fire against which it burned. He watched the
    wings
Drip coral flame, the breast grow lambent, darken, the dens
    bright hard body
Sheathe itself in the blue, become a remote speck, reappear
    upon its foreseen circle
Until his eyes blurred; he became afraid when his eyes blurred;
Perhaps he would be punished for looking on this thing . . .
    perhaps the World would take away
That dancing, soundless image of itself that grimaced with its
    mowing lips and trees that gibbered without noise . . .
He thought of darkness . . . great black wings flapping . . .
    flapping . . . and climbed hurriedly from the tree.
The man with his back to the rock hailed him with a feeble
    shout, Water, little brother, bring me water!
At the moment the boy, stretching his cramped limbs,
    turned,
Saw the gaunt head like a wounded bull's, the shoulders' beaten
    brass, the flies . . .
Aye, look well at me, I am Tiro, image maker of Sicily
Who was slave of Saius, captain of Pilate's guard — hast heard
    Saius is meat for the dogs?

The boy drew nearer, smiling a faint pleased smile; he was
  watching intently
The motions of the big brown hands threshing at the flies;
  To-day I'd have led the slaves
I — Tiro! Boy, boy, that dream is pricked . . . I delayed
  too long, too long . . . it was He
Who wrought this change in me — He who made my will sick.
  He wrote on my heart with stylus of fire
All men are brothers . . . He bade me love them that did hate
  me and despitefully use me . . . why did his eyes
Pick me out of the crowd to rest on and befool me with their
  soft shining.
When I went forth out of the Temple, bearing a tray of sugared
  fruits unto the house of Saius — the first star
Was big over Mount Moriah — I seemed to fold the evening in
  my arms,
I took hold of the wind, I trod
Gently on the dark body of the earth, patient, patient like a
  black slave-woman's . . .
They did follow him in hundreds, slaves and women . . .
  could 'st see plain from the tree top —
Did his lips move? The boy's large gentle eyes were fixed on
  him with a remote absorption;
Speak, speak, is there no tongue in thy head? Water, little
  he-goat, bring me water;

But in a moment he had forgotten.   Too late . . . I did wait
   too long . . . His eyes yellow as flame, roved over the
   cupped hills,

He played on men as they were harps . . . and they had music
   in them it did sound

Or silence or the discord of their strings . . . in me was a
   weak rotten spot He found . . .

My heart grew soft as a too ripe fruit . . . now it hath
   sloughed from off its stone . . . stone . . .

The stone is here.   He smote his chest over the wound, whose
   thickened rims

Opened like a mouth; the gaze of the boy became mildly rapt;

The place . . . the dry hot place . . . they tore out marbles
   for their images — I too

Gutted of precious things.   He stared wildly about him.   Faces

On the stones, amid the brambles, up in the cypress, faces

With outstanding ears and large observant eyes . . . listening
   . . . listening . . .

Brothers ! — His voice that had been as the drone of flies that
   browsed upon his wound

Blared like a trumpet — words are not enough unless they be
   cased in iron,

Hammered in bronze, beaten to broadswords; He did die that
   his words had not been dipped

In metal molten, He was a man unarmed.

Arm, glass-blowers, weavers of linen!

Bring axes, carpenters — saw chisel plane awl —

Anything of a sharp edge or whetted point. Let not his words

Make your hearts uneasy. He was our Brother, but He loved
too many;

He raised up the rich man's daughter when she was all but
dead; she had been one the less.

He did not know all things; neither John the Baptist — did not
John

Say unto the soldiers, be content with your pay. Messiah . . .
all Judea waiting for Messiah

To lead them . . . lead them, where . . . they did not know
him . . . He was a different

Jew . . . He was a man dangerous to governments, a despiser
of rules, making a mockery of ordinance . . .

Get up, paraders, leave your inn-feasts, freedmen — ye may be
slaves to-morrow, for in them is no safety.

Slaves, arise as ye did years back in the mines of Laurium,
seize the white stuff called silver,

White crop of the black pits they buy and sell us by. Why
tarry ye, think ye the Romans

Who will not let you serve in the legions shall gird on you
their swords?

I have made images

In ivory, brass, amber, I have inlaid with precious stones

Furrows of the dark wood . . . they said make unto us a
god . . . and I builded about the hollow of their dream
My dream that was alive and glowing . . . it is my gods they
have adored . . . mine . . . mine . . .
Bronze workers, cutters and carriers — ye dragging god-tim-
bers along hot trails
Where daylights, ground between the desert and the sky
Into a diamond dust, do with the air conspire
A fiery treason upon breath — shall we yet fashion gods for
our rulers
They even as the barren woman and we with the god-seed in
us?
Not of the sum of their fires but of our fires
Those figures of gold and iron and marbles with the sly smiles
sweet and terrible —
Break apart their gods and the pedestals of their gods, tear
down their temples!
Yet hesitate ye, million-footed?
But I say unto you there shall be made no wings great enough
to sustain our victories.
Silent . . . listening with their eyes . . . big eyes . . . not
of the blond skin . . . is it that I am not
Of the blond skin . . . Sit still then, ye gelded and about to be
gelded,
Await the first glint of the tool, sanded to an edge;

Hold your foreheads in place for the iron made hot; let the
  gray lungs of hills
Upspit ye with their broken silvers! What is it ye signal with
  your fingers . . . thousands of little fingers?
Is it that I get up and lead you — I, Tiro, with my back
  against a rock here in this hollow of the hills?
Await ye a saviour? I say ye have had too many saviours.
These things we have greatly done — vast walls, long roads —
By which they set our crucified — temples and palaces, we
  have wrought
With our arms together moving as one arm. Doth not the sea
Advance with all her crested company. The sea
Hath dancers . . . shapes of foam that banner in the light . . .
  our oars . . . shattering the moonlight on the Euphrates
  . . . moon on the slipping decks . . .
Doubt not that ye too shall have your leaders —
Ye shall be ridden who do arch your backs . . .
Think ye to lose your corner of a mean room, not a curtain
Between ye who would embrace your mates or before the
  woman bringing forth her babe —
Ye, sleepers on filthy floors and scorpions
Crawling through the crevices — ye drinking fouled water
  and sour wines . . . men say the goblets of Murrah
Do flavour the draught as a flower the raindrops it holds within
  its cup . . .

O for a long cool drink . . . cool, cooled of high snows . . .

Water, water — is not there a one among ye shall bring me
water? the boy

Saw the mouth drawn back and up from the white perfect
teeth, the eyes, amber as a lion's, glazing

And thought vaguely of water, water, running over greeny-
gold pebbles

He half arose, saw but the rocks, the glittering sand, settled
back upon his stone.

Tiro was saying, Speak no more evil one of the other; if He —
who did speak no evil,

Neither in the temple nor on the high road nor in the small
room in the inn

Nor on the rims of cornfields, there gathered with two or three,

Nor under the wild rose nor on the fallen log where He did lay
his head —

Was yet betrayed by his own friend, by how many more shall
ye,

Defamers and little haters, lacking the love of brothers,

Be beset by your Iscariots. Love . . . is for a moment, a
flash that shineth and then is not . . .

Faces . . . faces . . . clapping of little hands. Do you applaud me, brothers?

They commanded and we sang. Not our song but their song
our anonymous

Lips trumpeted in stone . . . we sang their brave deeds and
their heroes . . .

Have we not too our heroes whereof no man singeth

Save a slave in secret among other slaves . . . my grandfather

Made songs about Athenion . . . Athenion rode forth with
his herdsmen.

Brothers, ye have been patient, ye sitting still for a long while,
not turning your heads to right nor left,

I am happy ye shall carry off my words in your hearts . . . I
was afraid

I had waited too long . . . numbers on infinite numbers . . .

Out of the chasms . . . out of the hymning clay . . . who
art thou, coming up the limestone path? Thy sleeve

Maketh a shining in the brambles. Put forth thy hand to me
that I may get up on my feet,

I am a sick man . . . He did not look on me . . . He hath
passed by, not turning this way . . .

2.

T'is growing dark . . . the brambles silver . . . I am
a strong man, hard to kill . . . Saius
Did look at me with strange eyes before he died.
There was wonder in them and a question.

He might have spoken an he would, but his word lay still in his
mouth . . . only his eyes

Stammered some thing, unclear as the writing on a stone

Made by a man far spent who dippeth his finger in his own
blood . . . an I did read aright it almost

Seemed he did not hate me any more . . . when I ran him
through for the second time . . . the look

Froze in his eyes . . . but it had reached my heart . . . broke
off there, leaving a fine point . . .

There is no hate left in me any more . . . is it my will

Dissolveth upon the twilight, making a stain there like a little
breath . . .

Brothers, ye will arise and be defeated and arise again . . .
your day shall come.

You will do unto them all these things which they have done
unto you, aye, and to each other . . .

All men . . . are brothers . . . a vast thread weaving and we
strung there on . . .

Rocks . . . curling into flames . . . the trees figures of flame
. . . I am a spot

Of coolness in all this fire raging upon the world, a still small
  pool
Of quietness . . . there is a great wheel slowed somewhere
  . . . Are ye all gone brothers, is there not one left?
Carriers of fire . . . who flee before the fire . . . I cannot see
  the cross
I think 'twas there, up on that blue blank wall of sky . . . there
  was a bird . . . the moon
Flowers over the Place . . .

IX

THE RESURRECTION

I.

I see him — ah, his thorns are bright!
And He hath pierced me with his light,
Who draweth me by my two hands
Unto the bow whereon He stands
The flaming arch whose colors span
The night, till there is no more night!

But ah, his thorns are sharp between,
He, whose waste love overpoured
The rigid confines of his word
And filled me, a predestined urn
In which the living sap might burn
To utter light and its pure ray
Shine on from me as from a star
When it hath burned itself away.

This is the child I bear of him
Who shook me, as doth wind a pyre,
Almost consumed before it came,
Whereon flesh that hath burned to the charrèd limb,
Reanimate with the old fire,
Doth rear from the recumbent ash
The living tendons of a flame;
This is the vision that I share,

This is my blood and this my flesh
I divide with all who hear —
He hath not perished, He doth live!
Against the dimmer arc of heaven,
He shineth with refulgent ray;
He is not dead He hath arisen,
A flame within a flame; and day
Is but the shadow of the light
Doth burn amid its darker air.

2.

John came to camels grazing
And stalwart cedars
Had battled many winds and bore unhewn
Crosses under their great armpits,
And moved toward the joined hills stretching
Like a rupture across the morning.

Light gathered under a tolerant wing
Litter of Jerusalem and the imperial
Hills of Judea, yet swaddled
In white mist as in fine linen.
Light, brooding on the Mount he loved

Discovered his bright hair and blew
A golden horn among the olive trees
Wherein he, as a lost falcon
Cut off from the divine wrist
Did wander aimlessly.

Winged things arose, glistened and disappeared
Amid the plumbless jasmine of the light.
He passed a hamlet,
And noted the pale face of a woman
Some transient sorrow whitened
As moons silver the Dead Sea
Leaving their deeps unstirred;
He inhaled copiously
The air, sweet-savoured as a goat's milk
And facing the passivity of hills
Yearned for the enormous presence of the sea.
He heard
The endless banalities of water,
A foal whimper and afar off an ass bray,
Palms . . . making their foolish clatter;
There was no least thing deflected
In the cool routine of the day
That was perfect, as light carried,
And glistering without flaw.

He felt estranged, before this unchecked momentum of all
   things,
From the day peacefully grazing and the lowing hills,
And looked timidly upon the Marys,
Feeling even these remote, whose roots were as the mountains
And went down into rich and endless darkness;
They too dark-willed and secret
Like hills kneeling above their jewels —
They had no hunger for the light,
No unappeasable abiding need
For which to pour themselves as hills do lava.

So he moved, cut off from some essential root
Until at his stripped heart, now confineless
And utterly without defence there came
A lustrous swift touch as when a ray
Reaches for the first time a pool about whose brink
The over-leaning rushes have been torn:

     It lay so soft upon the hills
     He half divined a nimbus there,
     As men surmise a star, by day,
     In seamless light invisible,
     And yet . . . he could not know.

     The very stones upon the road
     Were not as they had been before;

They seemed to shed a certain glow,
As though each lambent particle
Had broke from out its stubborn cell
And glimmered through a door
Wherein the ray hid, tremulous,
Eluding those who pondered it —
Save a young child looked through
Who did not wonder that he knew
A stone's heart was luminous.

Not one whose feet were light on grass
As a breeze passing over
But one who wrestled with all winds
And bore each blade down as a lover
Till more than dew was pressed from it,
Had heard, as in a hollowed reed
The sound that threaded silverly
The casual sounds of things.

He felt the searching music pour
In through each ardent aperture
Till all the flesh's openings
Had closed upon it as a door
Might, in the chamber of a king,
On some bright lady entered there
To keep the kiss inviolate.

217

He stood apart, yet rimmed about
By the common luster of the air,
There at the hollow of the flame
He felt the self of music stir
Transfuse into the light . . . and then
A wand of fire immaculate
Light tremble into sound again,
Till his heart stumbled on a beat and fell —
Out of that radiant company
Out of the glory imperishable
And the shining without end . . .

The little heart that had run lame
And sank . . . to watch the flame ascend . . .

For none who heard might hold it long —
That silver singing underneath
The diapason of the sun
That sounded on Jerusalem,
Where encased in light as in a sheath
The star of morning sang with him
Who blent with morning's song.